ANNIE LENNOX

All The Top 40 Hits

Craig Halstead

Copyright © Craig Halstead 2020

All rights reserved. No part of this publication may be reproduced, stored in a retrieval system, or transmitted in any form or by any means, electronic, mechanical, photocopy, recording or otherwise, without prior written permission of the copyright owner. Nor can it be circulated in any form of binding or cover other than that in which it is published and without similar condition including this condition being imposed on a subsequent purchaser.

First Edition

for Aaron

BY THE SAME AUTHOR

Christmas Number Ones

This book details the Christmas No.1 singles in the UK from 1940 to date, and also reveals the Christmas No.2 single and Christmas No.1 album. The book also features the Christmas No.1s in five other countries, namely Australia, Germany, Ireland, the Netherlands and the USA, and is up-dated annually in January.

The 'All The Top 40 Hits' Series

This series documents, in chronological order, all the Top 40 Hit Singles and Albums by the featured artist:

ABBA
Blondie
Boney M.
Carpenters
Donna Summer
Janet Jackson
Michael Jackson
Olivia Newton-John
Whitney Houston

Top 40 Music Videos are also detailed in the Janet Jackson & Michael Jackson books.

The 'For The Record' Series

The books in this series are more comprehensive than the 'All The Top 40 Hits' volumes, and typically include: The Songs (released & unreleased), The Albums, The Home Videos, The TV Shows/Films, The Concerts, Chartography & USA/UK Chart Runs, USA Discography & UK Discography.

Donna Summer
Janet Jackson
Michael Jackson
Whitney Houston

ACKNOWLEDGEMENTS

I would like to thank Chris Cadman, my former writing partner, for helping to make my writing dreams come true. It's incredible to think how far we both have come, since we got together to compile 'The Complete Michael Jackson Discography 1972-1990', for Adrian Grant's *Off the Wall* fan magazine in 1990. Good luck with your ongoing projects, Chris ~ I will look forward to reading them in due course!

I would like to thank the online music community, who so readily share and exchange information at: ukmix (ukmix.org/forums), Haven (fatherandy2.proboards.com) & Buzzjack (buzzjack.com/forums). In particular, I would like to thank:

- 'BrainDamagell' & 'Wayne' for posting current Canadian charts on ukmix;
- 'flatdeejay' & 'ChartFreaky' for posting German chart action, and 'Indi' and 'vdoerken' for answering my queries regarding Germany, on ukmix;
- 'mario' for posting Japanese chart action, and 'danavon' for answering my queries regarding Japan, on ukmix;
- 'Davidalic' for posting Spanish chart action on ukmix;
- 'Shakyfan', 'CZB', 'trebor' & 'beatlened' for posting Irish charts on ukmix;
- 'grendizer' for posting Canadian certifications on ukmix;
- 'janjensen' for posting Danish singles charts from 1979 onwards on ukmix;
- 'Hanboo' for posting and up-dating on request full UK & USA chart runs on ukmix. R.I.P., Hanboo ~ like everyone on ukmix, I was shocked and deeply saddened to learn of your passing.

If you can fill any of the gaps in the chart information in this book, or have chart runs from a country not already featured in the book, I would love to hear from you. You can contact me via email at: **craig.halstead2@ntlworld.com** ~ thank you!

CONTENTS

INTRODUCTION	7
ALL THE TOP 40 SINGLES	19
THE ALMOST TOP 40 SINGLES	122
ANNIE'S TOP 30 SINGLES	124
SINGLES TRIVIA	128
ALL THE TOP 40 ALBUMS	143
ANNIE'S TOP 20 ALBUMS	222
ALBUMS TRIVIA	224

INTRODUCTION

Ann Lennox was born in Aberdeen, Scotland, on Christmas Day in 1954. She was the daughter of Thomas Allison Lennox and Dorothy Farquharson (nee Ferguson).

In the 1970s, Annie studied flute, harpsicord and piano at London's Royal Academy of Music, but to the dismay of her parents she dropped out just weeks before she finished her course. In 1976, she was the flute player with Dragon's Playground, but she left the band before they appeared on the popular British TV talent show, *New Faces*.

'It was Stevie Wonder who actually turned her (Annie) on to singing,' Dave Stewart confirmed. 'She was totally into being a flute player in a classical orchestra until she heard that album (*TALKING BOOK*) for the first time.'

'It was such a revelation to me to listen with very heightened senses to that record,' said Annie. 'It was an extraordinary experience to me at the time … It was something that in the future I wanted to aspire to, that kind of depth of subtlety and profound statement through music.'

Later in 1976, Annie met singer-songwriter Peet Coombes and guitarist David A. Stewart in London, and together they formed a trio called The Catch. Signed to Logo Records, the trio released a single, *Borderline* b/w *Black Blood*, in early 1977, in a limited number of countries, including the Netherlands, Portugal and Spain, as well as the UK, but it wasn't a hit.

When the trio were joined by bass guitarist Eddie Chin and drummer Jim Toomey, the new line-up renamed themselves The Tourists, and went on to release three studio albums, *THE TOURISTS* (1979), *REALITY EFFECT* (1979) and *LUMINOUS BASEMENT* (1980). All three albums charted in the UK, but only *REALITY EFFECT* ~ boosted by the success of the band's cover of Dusty Springfield's hit, *I Only Want To Be With You* ~ achieved Top 40 status.

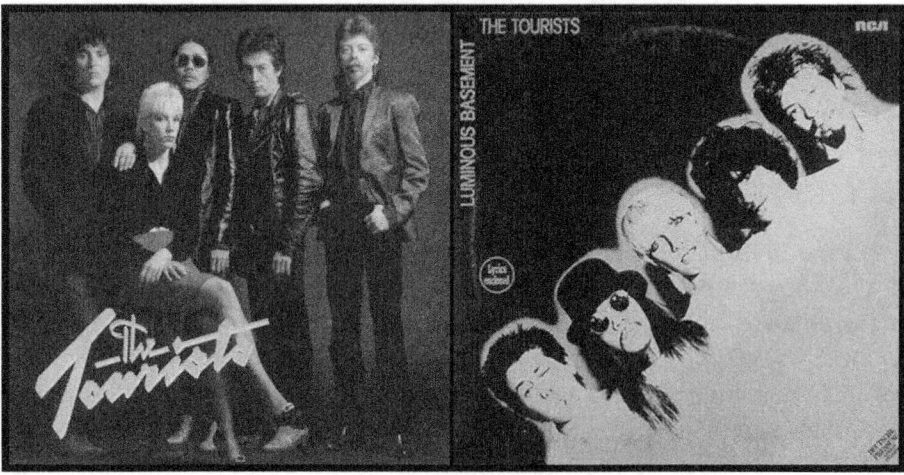

Having toured the UK and Ireland in September and October 1980, The Tourists flew to Thailand, and then on to Australia. However, on arrival in Sydney, Peet Coombes' drug habit saw him overdosing, and he returned to the UK to recuperate.

As well as being the main songwriter, Coombes' vocal contribution to the band was also important, and on returning to the UK the remaining band members faced a stark choice: carry on without Coombes, or split. They agreed to split, and go their separate ways.

By this time, Annie and fellow band member Dave Stewart were a couple. They decided to stay together and form a duo, which they named Eurythmics, after the Dalcroze eurythmics system of teaching music to students that Annie had encountered as a child.

Annie and Dave wrote and produced *IN THE GARDEN*, the debut album by Eurythmics, which was released in October 1981. Conny Plank co-produced the album, and Roger Pomphrey co-wrote two tracks, *English Summer* and *Caveman Head*. The album wasn't a hit anywhere.

Two singles were released from *IN THE GARDEN*, *Never Gonna Cry Again* and *Belinda*. *Never Gonna Cry Again* was a minor no.63 hit in the UK, but *Belinda* failed to chart anywhere.

Eurythmics released their second album, *SWEET DREAMS (ARE MADE OF THIS)*, in January 1983 and, initially at least, it proved no more successful than *IN THE GARDEN*.

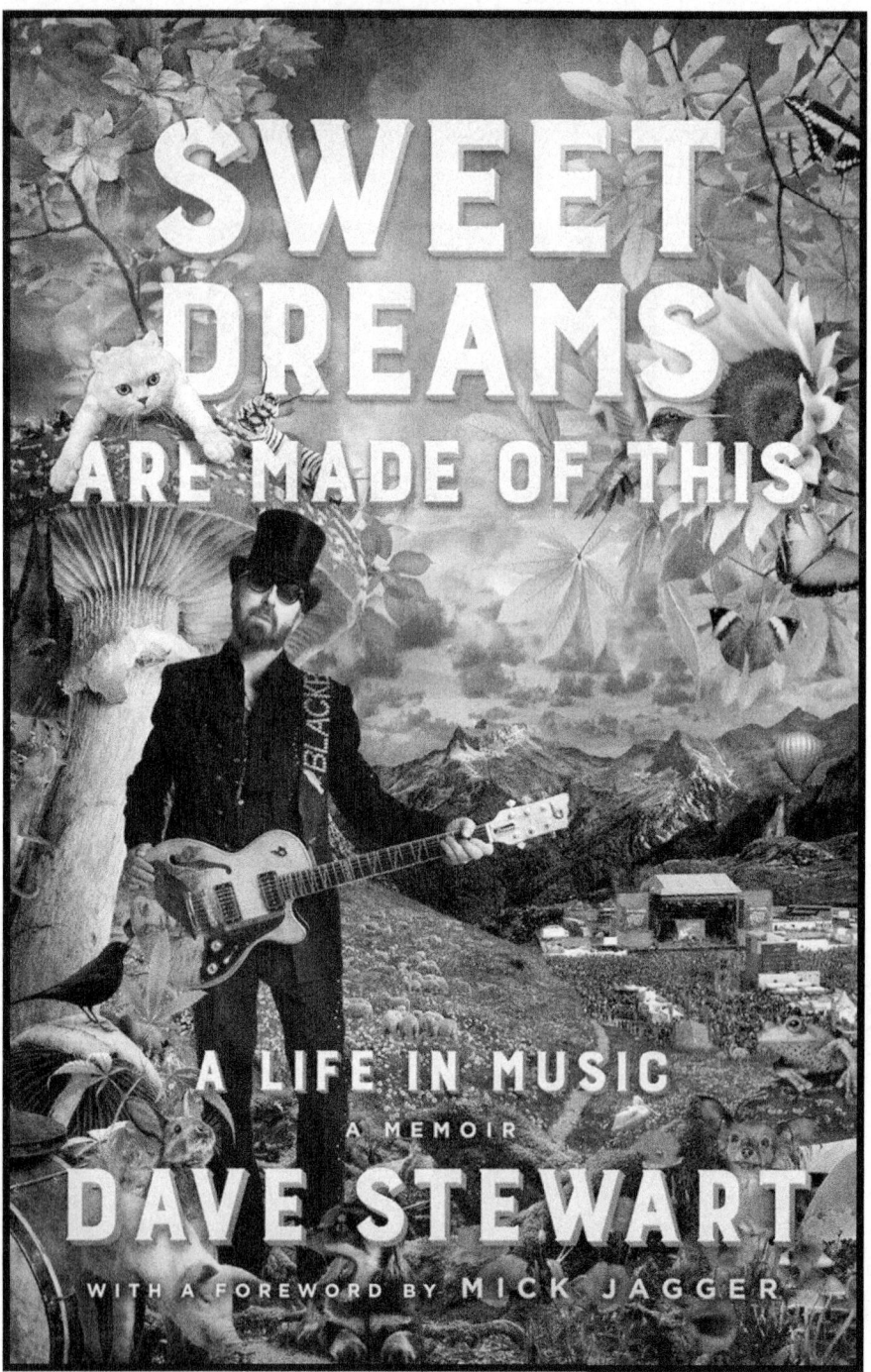

The first two singles, *This Is The House* and *The Walk*, were released in 1982 but the former failed to chart anywhere, and *The Walk* could only manage no.89 in the UK.

The album's third single, *Love Is A Stranger*, was a minor no.54 hit in the UK, and it became the duo's first Top 40 success when it climbed to no.12 in Germany in early 1983.

However, it wasn't until the album's title track was issued as the fourth single, that Eurythmics finally made their name around the world, and the success of *Sweet Dreams (Are Made Of This)* led to *Love Is A Stranger* enjoying belated chart success as well, as the duo's popularity quickly grew.

Between 1981-89, Eurythmics released seven studio albums, but serious disagreements between Annie and Dave led to the duo disbanding in 1990. While Annie took time off to have a baby and reflect on life after Eurythmics, Dave Stewart involved himself in writing film music, most notably the hit *Lily Was Here*, which he recorded with saxophonist Candy Dulfer, for the Dutch movie, *De Kassière*.

Dave Stewart also formed a band, The Spiritual Cowboys, which released two albums, *DAVE STEWART & THE SPIRITUAL COWBOYS* in 1990 and *HONEST* in 1991. Dave Stewart's autobiography, *Sweet Dreams Are Made Of This – A Life In Music*, was published in 2016.

Annie resumed her career in music in 1992, when she released her debut solo album, *DIVA*, which proved a commercial and critical success. To date, she had released six solo studio albums and one compilation, her most recent being *NOSTALGIA* in 2014. Annie and Dave Stewart reunited as Eurythmics in 1999, issuing a new album titled *PEACE*, and embarking on a global 'Peacetour'.

Annie has picked up eight BRIT Awards over the years, including being named Best British Female Artist six times. Solo and with Eurythmics, she has won four Grammy Awards:

- 1987: Best Rock Performance by a Duo or Group with Vocal ~ *Missionary Man*
- 1993: Album of the Year ~ *DIVA*
- 1996: Best Pop Vocal Performance, Female ~ *No More "I Love You's"*
- 2005: Best Song Written for Visual Media ~ *Into The West*

Annie co-wrote *Into The West* with Fran Walsh and Howard Shore, and performed it as the end-credits song for the 2003 film, *The Lords Of The Rings: The Return Of The King*. As well as picking up a Grammy, *Into The West* also won a Golden Globe Award and an Academy Award, as Best Original Song.

In recognition of her 'tireless charity campaigns and championing of humanitarian causes', Annie was awarded an OBE (Order of the British Empire) in 2011.

All The Top 40 Hits

For the purposes of this book, to qualify as a Top 40 hit, a single or album must have entered the Top 40 singles/albums chart in at least one of the following featured countries: Australia, Austria, Belgium (Flanders), Canada, Denmark, Finland, France, Germany, Ireland (singles only), Japan, Netherlands, New Zealand, Norway, South Africa (singles only), Spain, Sweden, Switzerland, United Kingdom, United States of America and Zimbabwe.

The Top 40 singles and albums are detailed chronologically, according to the date they first entered the chart in one or more of the featured countries. Each Top 40 single and album is illustrated and catalogue numbers and release dates are detailed for the UK, followed by the chart runs in each featured country, including any chart re-entries. Where full chart runs are unavailable, peak position and weeks on the chart are given.

For both singles and albums, the main listing is followed by 'The Almost Top 40 Singles/Albums', which gives an honourable mention to singles/albums that peaked between no.41 and no.50 in one or more countries. There is also a points-based list of Annie's most successful singles and albums, plus a fascinating 'Trivia' section at the end of each section which looks at the most successful singles and albums in each of the featured countries.

The Charts

The charts from an increasing number of countries are now freely available online, and for many countries it is possible to research weekly chart runs. Although this book focuses on Top 40 hits, longer charts runs are included where available, up to the Top 100 for countries where a Top 100 or longer is published. Where full chart runs are unavailable, peak positions and weeks on the chart are detailed.

Nowadays, charts are compiled and published on a weekly basis. In the past, however, some countries published charts on a bi-weekly or monthly basis, and most charts listed far fewer titles than they do today. There follows a summary of the current charts from each country featured in this book, together with relevant online resources and chart books.

Australia
Current charts: Top 100 Singles & Top 100 Albums.
Online resources: current weekly Top 50 Singles & Albums, but no archive, at **ariacharts.com.au**; archive of complete weekly charts dating back to 2001 at **pandora.nla.gov.au/tep/23790**; searchable archive of Top 50 Singles & Albums dating back to 1988 at **australian-charts.com**.
Books: 'Australian Chart Book 1970-1992' & 'Australian Chart Book 1993-2009' by David Kent.

Austria
Current charts: Top 75 Singles & Top 75 Albums.
Online resources: current weekly charts and a searchable archive dating back to 1965 for singles and 1973 for albums at **austriancharts.at**.

Belgium (Flanders)
Current charts: Top 50 Singles & Top 200 Albums.
Online resources: current weekly charts and a searchable archive (albums dating back to 1995 only) at **ultratop.be/nl/**.

Canada
Current charts: Hot 100 Singles & Top 100 Albums.
Online resources: weekly charts and a searchable archive of weekly charts from the Nielsen SoundScan era at **billboard.com/biz** (subscription only); incomplete archive of weekly RPM charts dating back to 1964 for singles and 1967 for albums at **bac-lac.gc.ca/eng/discover/films-videos-sound-recordings/rpm/Pages/rpm.aspx** (RPM folded in 2000); weekly charts are posted on **ukmix.org**.
Book: 'The Canadian Singles Chart Book 1975-1996' by Nanda Lwin.
Note: due to the patchy nature of the RPM archive, the information for singles in this book is taken from Nanda Lwin's book.

Denmark
Current Charts: Top 40 Singles & Albums.
Online resources: weekly charts dating back to 2001 at **hitlisten.nu**. In 2001, the chart was a weekly Top 20, which expanded to a Top 40 in November 2007. No archive currently exists for charts before 2001. 'CZB' has posted weekly Top 20s from September 1994 to December 1999 on **ukmix.org**, and 'janjensen' has posted singles charts from January 1979 to 2000 on the same forum. This means no album charts before September 1994 are available.

Finland
Current charts: Top 20 Singles & Top 50 Albums.
Online resources: current weekly charts and a searchable archive dating back to 1995 at **finnishcharts.com**.
Book: *Sisältää Hitin* by Timo Pennanem.

France
Current charts: Top 200 Singles Albums.
Online resources: current weekly charts at **snepmusique.com**, plus weekly charts and a searchable archive dating back to 1984 for singles and 1997 for albums at **lescharts.com**; searchable archive for earlier/other charts at **infodisc.fr**.
Book: '*Hit Parades 1950-1998*' by Daniel Lesueur.
Note: Compilation albums were excluded from the main chart until 2008, when a Top 200 Comprehensive chart was launched.

Germany
Current charts: Top 100 Singles & Top 100 Albums.
Online resources: current weekly charts and a searchable archive dating back to 1977 at **offizellecharts.de**; Top 10s only and a searchable archive dating back to 2007 (again, Top 10s only) at **germancharts.com**.
Books: '*Deutsche Chart Singles 1956-1980*', '*Deutsche Chart Singles 1981-90*', '*Deutsche Chart Singles 1991-1995*' & '*Deutsche Chart LP's 1962-1986*' published by Taurus Press.

Ireland
Current charts: Top 100 Singles & Top 100 Albums.
Online resources: current weekly charts are published at IRMA (**irma.ie**); there is a searchable archive for Top 30 singles (entry date, peak position and week on chart only) at **irishcharts.ie**; an annual Irish Chart Thread has been published annually from 2007 to date, plus singles charts from 1967 to 1999 and album charts for 1993, 1995-6 and 1999, have been published at ukmix (**ukmix.org**); weekly album charts from March 2003 to date can be found at **acharts.us/ireland_albums_top_75**.
Note: the information presented in this book is for singles only.

Japan
Current charts: Top 200 Singles & Top 300 Albums.
Online resources: current weekly charts (in Japanese) at **oricon.co.jp/rank**; selected information is available on the Japanese Chart/The Newest Charts and Japanese Chart/The Archives threads at **ukmix.org**.

Netherlands
Current charts: Top 100 Singles & Top 100 Albums.
Online resources: current weekly charts and a searchable archive dating back to 1956 for singles and 1969 for albums at **dutchcharts.nl**.

New Zealand
Current charts: Top 40 Singles & Top 40 Albums.
Online resources: current weekly charts and archive charts dating back to 1975 at **nztop40.co.nz**.
Book: 'The Complete New Zealand Music Charts 1966-2006' by Dean Scapolo.

Norway
Current charts: Top 20 Singles & Top 40 Albums.
Online resources: current weekly charts and a searchable archive dating back to 1958 for singles and 1967 for albums at **norwegiancharts.com**.

South Africa
Current charts: no official charts.
Online resources: none known.

Book: 'South Africa Chart Book' by Christopher Kimberley.
Notes: the singles chart was discontinued in early 1989, as singles were no longer being manufactured in significant numbers. The albums chart only commenced in December 1981, and was discontinued in 1995, following re-structuring of the South African Broadcasting Corporation.

Spain
Current charts: Top 50 Singles & Top 100 Albums.
Online resources: current weekly charts and a searchable archive dating back to 2005 at **spanishcharts.com**.
Book: *'Sólo éxitos 1959-2002 Año a Año'* by Fernando Salaverri.

Sweden
Current charts: Top 60 Singles & Top 100 Albums.
Online resources: current weekly charts and a searchable archive dating back to 1975 at **swedishcharts.com**.

Switzerland
Current charts: Top 75 Singles & Top 100 Albums.
Online resources: current weekly charts and a searchable archive dating back to 1968 for singles and 1983 for albums at **hitparade.ch**.

UK
Current Charts: Top 100 Singles & Top 200 Albums.
Online resources: current weekly Top 100 charts and a searchable archive dating back to 1960 at **officialcharts.com**; weekly charts are posted on a number of music forums, including ukmix (**ukmix.org**), Haven (**fatherandy2.proboards.com**) and Buzzjack (**buzzjack.com**).
Note: weekly Top 200 albums charts are only available via subscription from UK ChartsPlus (**ukchartsplus.co.uk**).

USA
Current charts: Hot 100 Singles & Billboard 200 Albums.
Online resources: current weekly charts are available at **billboard.com**, however, to access Billboard's searchable archive at **billboard.com/biz** you must be a subscriber; weekly charts are posted on a number of music forums, including ukmix (**ukmix.org**), Haven (**fatherandy2.proboards.com**) and Buzzjack (**buzzjack.com**).
Note: older 'catalog' albums (i.e. albums older than two years) were excluded from the Billboard 200 before December 2009, so the chart didn't accurately reflect the country's best-selling albums. Therefore, in this book Billboard's Top Comprehensive Albums chart has been used from December 2003 to December 2009, as this did include all albums. In December 2009 the Top Comprehensive Albums chart became the Billboard 200, and Billboard launched a new Top Current Albums chart – effectively, the old Billboard 200.

Zimbabwe
Current charts: no official charts.
Online resources: none known.
Books: 'Zimbabwe Singles Chart Book' by Christopher Kimberley.
Note: Zimbabwe was, of course, known as Rhodesia before 1980, but the country is referred to by its present name throughout this book.

Note: In the past, there was often one or more weeks over Christmas and New Year when no new album chart was published in some countries. In such cases, the previous week's chart has been used to complete a chart run. Similarly, where a bi-weekly or monthly chart was in place, for chart runs these are counted at two and four weeks, respectively.

All The Top 40 Singles

1 ~ The Loneliest Man In The World by The Tourists

UK: Logo GO 360 (1979).
  B-side: *Don't Get Left Behind*.

8.09.79: 72-50-45-40-35-**32**-53

The Loneliest Man In The World was the second and last single released from The Tourists' debut, self-titled album. The song was written by the band's Peet Coombes, although the BMI database also credits Annie Lennox and Dave Stewart (the record label itself only credits Coombes).

The single gave The Tourists their first Top 40 hit in the UK, where it rose to no.32, twenty places higher than the band's debut single, *Blind Among The Flowers*. However, the single wasn't a hit anywhere else.

The Loneliest Man In The World was issued as a 7" picture disc in the UK only.

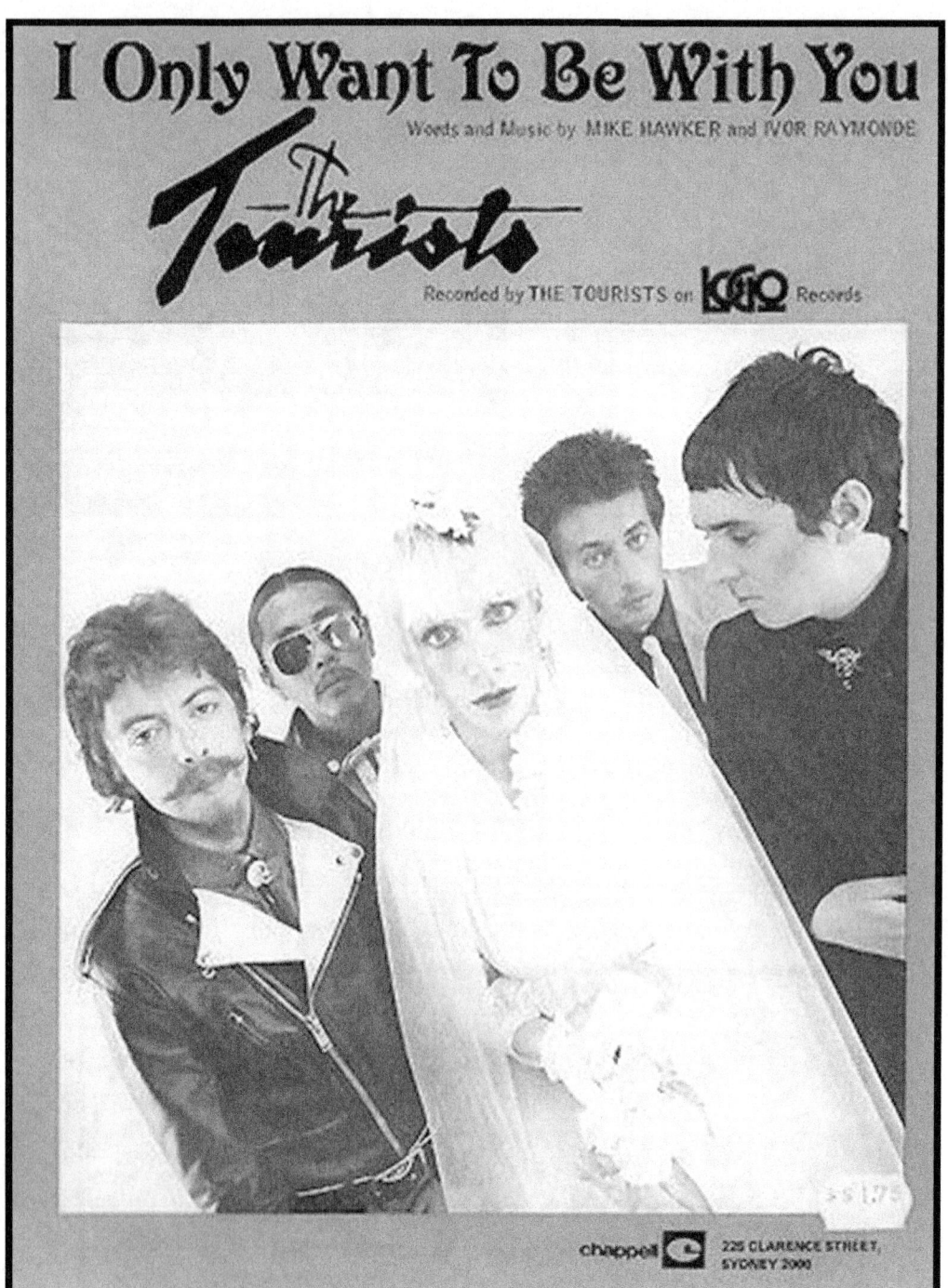

2 ~ I Only Want To Be With You by The Tourists

UK: Logo GO 370 (1979).
  B-side: *Summers Night*.

10.11.79: 75-43-28-22-6-**4**-5-5-4-5-10-25-38-67

Australia
9.06.80: peaked at no.**6**, charted for 19 weeks

Ireland
16.12.79: **13**-14-14-**13**-**13**-17-19

USA
17.05.80: 87-87-**83**-92

I Only Want To Be With You was composed by Mike Hawker and Ivor Raymonde, and was originally recorded by Dusty Springfield in 1963 for her album, *STAY AWHILE – I ONLY WANT TO BE WITH YOU*. Released as a single, Dusty's recording charted at no.4 in the UK, no.6 in Australia, no.7 in Ireland and New Zealand, and no.12 in the USA.

The Tourists recorded a cover of *I Only Want To Be With You* for their second album, 1979's *REALITY EFFECT*. The track was chosen as the album's lead single, and gave the band their biggest hit to date ~ it achieved no.4 in the UK (the same as Dusty's original), no.6 in Australia (again, the same as Dusty's original), no.13 in Ireland and no.83 in the USA, where it proved to be the band's only chart success.

The success of *I Only Want To Be With You* left Annie and Dave Stewart with mixed feelings.

'We rose to fame on a song that came out almost by accident,' said Annie. 'We did it so casually at the time, but the press absolutely slaughtered us … We were taken to the bloody cleaners for doing that bloody song and I swear to you we were not jumping on a bandwagon … It drove me mad, it really wasn't wholly representative of the rest of the music.'

Dave Stewart concurred, saying, 'The throwaway fun songs became phenomenally successful, that's all ~ so what can you do?'

There have been numerous versions of *I Only Want To Be With You* recorded over the years, with both the Bay City Rollers and Samantha Fox also recording hit versions (re-titled *I Only Wanna Be With You*).

The Bay City Rollers version, released in 1976, charted at no.2 in Ireland, no.4 in the UK, no.8 in Australia, no.9 in Germany and the Netherlands, and no.12 in New Zealand and the USA. This meant, of course, Dusty Springfield, The Tourists and the Bay City Rollers had all scored a no.4 hit in the UK with the same song.

Samantha Fox's 1989 cover *I Only Wanna Be With You* achieved no.9 in Ireland, no.13 in the Netherlands, no.16 in the UK, no.19 in Australia, no.25 in Germany and no.31 in the USA.

3 ~ So Good To Be Back Home Again by The Tourists

UK: Logo TOUR 1 (1979).
  B-side: *Circular Fever*.

9.02.80: 46-18-10-**8**-11-19-37-62-71

Ireland
3.03.80: **9**-13

So Good To Be Back Home Again was written by Peet Coombes, and recorded by The Tourists for their 1979 album, *REALITY EFFECT*.
  Issued as the follow-up to *I Only Want To Be With You*, *So Good To Be Back Home Again* gave the band their second Top 10 hit in the UK, where it peaked at no.8. The single also gave The Tourists their first Top 10 record in Ireland, achieving no.9, but it failed to chart in most countries and proved to be the band's final big hit.

4 ~ Don't Say I Told You So by The Tourists

UK: RCA TOUR 2 (1980).
B-side: *Strange Sky*.

18.10.80: 57-**40**-46-50-71

Composed by Peet Coombes, The Tourists recorded *Don't Say I Told You So* for their third and final studio album, 1980's *LUMINOUS BASEMENT*.

Don't Say I Told You So was released as the album's lead single and although it did, just, achieve Top 40 status in the UK, it wasn't a hit anywhere else.

The Tourists promoted *Don't Say I Told You So* and *LUMINOUS BASEMENT* with dates in the UK and Ireland in September and October 1980, before flying to Thailand and Australia. However, shortly after the band's arrival in Sydney, Peet Coombes overdosed, and was forced to fly back to the UK to recover.

The remaining band members honoured their commitments in Australia but, given Coombes was the band's primary songwriter and one of the band's main vocalists, they felt they couldn't continue without him, and on their return to the UK it was agreed to disband The Tourists.

5 ~ Love Is A Stranger by Eurythmics

UK: RCA PB 5525 / DA 1 (1982), RCA PB 44265 (1991).
  B-side (1982): *Monkey, Monkey*
  B-side (1991): *Julia*

13.11.82: 85-70-66-54-64-70-x-x-x-98
9.04.83: 49-23-**6**-7-12-17-31-52
9.03.91: 58-46-52

Australia
18.04.83: peaked at no.**17**, charted for 22 weeks

Belgium
11.06.83: 10-**6**-12-11-10-9-12-12-17-19-31

Canada
19.12.83: peaked at no.**25**, charted for 10 weeks

Germany
20.12.82: 64-71-75-67-62-73-29-37-37-**12-12**-14-**12**-15-17-20-24-30-33-40-52-53-52-69-73

Ireland
24.04.83: 15-**4**-5-26

Netherlands
4.06.83: 35-17-13-**12**-13-14-21-30

New Zealand
19.06.83: 42-34-23-21-21-22-28-**20**-22-21-30-31-36-33-41-40-43

South Africa
24.09.83: peaked at no.**2**, charted for 19 weeks

USA
17.09.83: 81-63-52-42-32-29-25-24-**23**-31-56-68-97

Annie co-wrote *Love Is A Stranger* with Dave Stewart (invariably credited as David A. Stewart or D.A. Stewart), and the duo co-produced the track with Adam Williams, and recorded it for the second Eurythmics album, *SWEET DREAMS (ARE MADE OF THIS)*. Kiki Dee, a friend of Dave Stewart, sang backing vocals on the recording.

'What I did was put opposites together,' said Annie, 'because love and hate are so close to each other. Instead of saying "It's the most wonderful thing that's ever happened to me", I put, "It's the most devastating thing that's ever happened to me".

Before *Love Is A Stranger*, Eurythmics had achieved two minor hit singles in the UK only, from their first four releases. Initially, it looked as if *Love Is A Stranger* would be another minor hit, when it peaked at no.54 in the UK. The single did rather better in Germany, eventually climbing to no.12 for three non-consecutive weeks, to give Eurythmics their first Top 40 success in early 1983.

The huge success of the follow-up, *Sweet Dreams (Are Made Of This)*, led to *Love Is A Stranger* being reissued. This time, it was much more successful, charting at no.2 in South Africa, no.4 in Ireland, no.6 in Belgium and the UK, no.12 in the Netherlands, no.17 in Australia, no.20 in New Zealand, no.23 in the USA and no.25 in Canada.

Love Is A Stranger was reissued for a second time in 1991, to promote the Eurythmics compilation, *GREATEST HITS*. Once again, the single entered the UK chart, but it peaked outside the Top 40 at no.46.

6 ~ Sweet Dreams (Are Made Of This) by Eurythmics

UK: RCA PB 68031 / DA 2 (1983), RCA PB 45031 (1991).
  B-side (1983): *I Could Give You (A Mirror)*.
  B-side (1991): *The King & Queen Of America*.

12.02.83: 63-38-21-5-3-**2**-3-5-5-15-25-33-50-60
16.11.91: 48-58   ('91 Remix)

Australia
16.05.83: peaked at no.**6**, charted for 19 weeks

Austria
15.08.83: **9**-11-11-18 (bi-weekly)

Belgium
16.04.83: 33-32-6-**3**-**3**-4-6-15-21-39

Canada
3.10.83: peaked at no.**1** (3), charted for 22 weeks

Finland
04.83: peaked at no.**8**, charted for 4 weeks (monthly)

France
4.03.06: **27**-29-36-38-41-45-54-61-75-86-97 (Remix)

Germany
18.04.83: 65-18-7-6-7-5-8-6-5-5-**4**-8-9-13-13-16-26-22-31-38-53-61-67

Ireland
13.03.83: 3-3-**2**-4-14

Japan
21.08.83: peaked at no.**89**, charted for 4 weeks

Netherlands
9.04.83: 34-19-13-**10**-13-24-23-34-39

New Zealand
10.07.83: 25-9-6-4-**2**-5-5-6-9-14-17-24-24-30-28-41-46

South Africa
21.05.83: peaked at no.**5**, charted for 14 weeks

Spain
14.11.83: peaked at no.**3**, charted for 16 weeks

Switzerland
22.05.83: 10-10-**8**-9-14

USA
14.05.83: 90-78-57-52-46-37-32-26-20-15-11-6-2-2-2-2-**1**-2-5-6-16-22-48-66-77-83

Zimbabwe
9.07.83: peaked at no.**8**, charted for 13 weeks

Annie and Dave Stewart co-wrote *Sweet Dreams (Are Made Of This)* soon after The Tourists spilt, and they formed Eurythmics. The lyrics were inspired by the break-up of The Tourists, when Annie felt they were in a dream world, at the same time feeling whatever they were chasing was never going to happen.

'I was feeling very vulnerable,' said Annie. 'The song was an expression of how I felt: hopeless and nihilistic.'

Annie and Dave recorded *Sweet Dreams (Are Made Of This)* at two small London home studios, one above a picture framing shop in the Chalk Farm district, and the other in a small room at The Church studios in North London. To purchase the necessary equipment, including a Tascam 8-track tape recorder, a Roland Space Echo keyboard and a Soundcraft mixer, Annie and Dave took out two banks loans, for £5,000 and £2,000.

'Dave and I almost split up the day we wrote *Sweet Dreams*,' said Annie. 'I'm very negative and he's very positive, but we were just having a terrible time and I couldn't take it anymore, and I said so ... I was lying on the floor, curled up in a foetal position and he programmed this (drum) rhythm. It sounded so good that in the end I couldn't resist it.'

Originally, the duo's record company RCA didn't see *Sweet Dreams (Are Made Of This)* as a potential single, as it didn't have an obvious chorus. However, when a Cleveland DJ persisted in playing it, locally the track's popularity grew and, following the lack of success of previous Eurythmics singles, RCA decided they had nothing to lose by releasing it. It proved to be a wise decision: *Sweet Dreams (Are Made Of This)* was the single that brought Eurythmics worldwide recognition.

Sweet Dreams (Are Made Of This) was the first Eurythmics single issued in North America. In the USA, after a slow start, it rose to no.2 on Billboard's Hot 100, where it spent four weeks behind *Every Breath You Take* by The Police, before finally rising to no.1. The single also went to no.1 in Canada, and achieved no.2 in Ireland, New Zealand and the UK, no.3 in Belgium and Spain, no.4 in Germany, no.5 in South Africa, no.6 in Australia, no.8 in Finland, Switzerland and Zimbabwe, no.9 in Austria and no.10 in the Netherlands.

'I would say *Sweet Dreams (Are Made Of This)* is one of the most important records of 1983,' said Dave Stewart. 'To us the lyrics are so cutting and poignant, and it's been very carefully structured. We're not interested in creating anything unless it's really powerful.'

Over the years, *Sweet Dreams (Are Made Of This)* has been reissued several times. In 1991, the track was remixed and reissued to promote the compilation, *GREATEST HITS*. The remix charted at no.48 in the UK, but failed to chart in most countries.

In 2006, a remix by Steve Angello charted at no.27 in France.

Marilyn Manson released a cover of *Sweet Dreams (Are Made Of This)*, titled simply *Sweet Dreams*, in 1996. His version charted at no.28 in Australia and no.50 in New Zealand, and was a minor hit in the UK.

Another cover, also titled *Sweet Dreams*, by JX Riders ft. Skylar Stecker went all the way to no.1 on Billboard's dance chart in 2016.

7 ~ Who's That Girl? by Eurythmics

UK: RCA PB 68075 / DA 3 (1983).
  B-side: *You Take Some Lentils ... And You Take Some Rice*.

9.07.83: 29-9-4-**3**-4-7-13-24-34-51

Australia
19.09.83: peaked at no.**20**, charted for 18 weeks

Belgium
6.08.83: 29-18-16-**14**-21

Canada
2.07.84: peaked at no.**18**, charted for 7 weeks

Germany
8.08.83: 31-28-**19**-20-23-29-43-48-52-68-75

Ireland
17.07.83: 24-6-**5**-9-14-12

Netherlands
6.08.83: 31-**30**-**30**-**30**-33-39-48

New Zealand
9.10.83: 31-19-**13**-17-20-17-23-26-36-31-30-30-30-30-30-32-30-28-35-40

EURYTHMICS

WHO'S THAT GIRL?

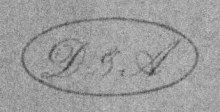

D & A

THE NEW SINGLE

*available on both 7" and 12"
in picture bags
12" features Special Bonus Track*
ABC(FREEFORM)

RCA

Sweden
9.08.83: **14**-17-x-16-17 (bi-weekly)

USA
5.05.84: 61-45-38-30-27-24-22-**21-21**-41-52-71-94

Who's That Girl? was composed by Annie and Dave Stewart, and recorded by Eurythmics for the due's third album, *TOUCH*.
 'With *Who's That Girl?*', said Annie, 'I was rather desperately in love at the time, and a lot of my songs were about unrequited love. At the time the songs meant only one thing to me, but at different times came to mean different things. Songs are quite organic.'
 Outside North America, *Who's That Girl?* was released as the album's lead single; in North America, it was issued as the second single, after *Here Comes The Rain Again*.
 Annie and Dave promoted *Who's That Girl?* with a music video in which Annie played several roles, including a nightclub singer and a member of the audience posing as Elvis Presley. Dave Stewart is seen escorting a number of female guests, including Kiki Dee, Hazel O'Connor, Kate Garner of Haysi Fantayzee, Cheryl Baker and Jay Aston of Bucks Fizz, and all four members of Bananarama, including Jacquie O'Sullivan, who replaced Dave's future wife-to-be, Siobhan Fahey.
 The music video enjoyed heavy rotation on MTV, which helped the single to no.3 in the UK, no.5 in Ireland, no.13 in New Zealand, no.14 in Belgium and Sweden, no.18 in Canada, no.19 in Germany, no.20 in Australia, no.21 in the USA and no.30 in the Netherlands.

SPIN

ANNIE LENNOX
WHO'S THAT GIRL?

MIDNIGHT OIL
GEORGE BURNS
DEE SNIDER
BILLY BRAGG
WEIRD AL YANKOVIC
SONIC YOUTH
GUADALCANAL DIARY

EXCLUSIVE:
IKE TURNER
WHAT IKE HAD
TO DO WITH IT:
THE FLIP SIDE
TO TINA'S STORY

8 ~ Right By Your Side by Eurythmics

UK: PB 68126 / DA 4 (1983).
  B-side: *Right By Your Side (Party Mix)*.

5.11.83: 45-27-23-15-**10**-14-19-28-28-31-42

Australia
26.12.83: peaked at no.**15**, charted for 18 weeks

Belgium
10.12.83: 36-**31**-33

Germany
5.12.83: 63-65-**61**-66-70

Ireland
20.11.83: 27-18-**15**-22

Netherlands
26.11.83: **31**-31-36-33-32-41-47-50

New Zealand
22.01.84: 39-12-**9**-22-17-32-34-34-50-43

Sweden
15.11.83: 18-**13**-x-x-19 (bi-weekly)

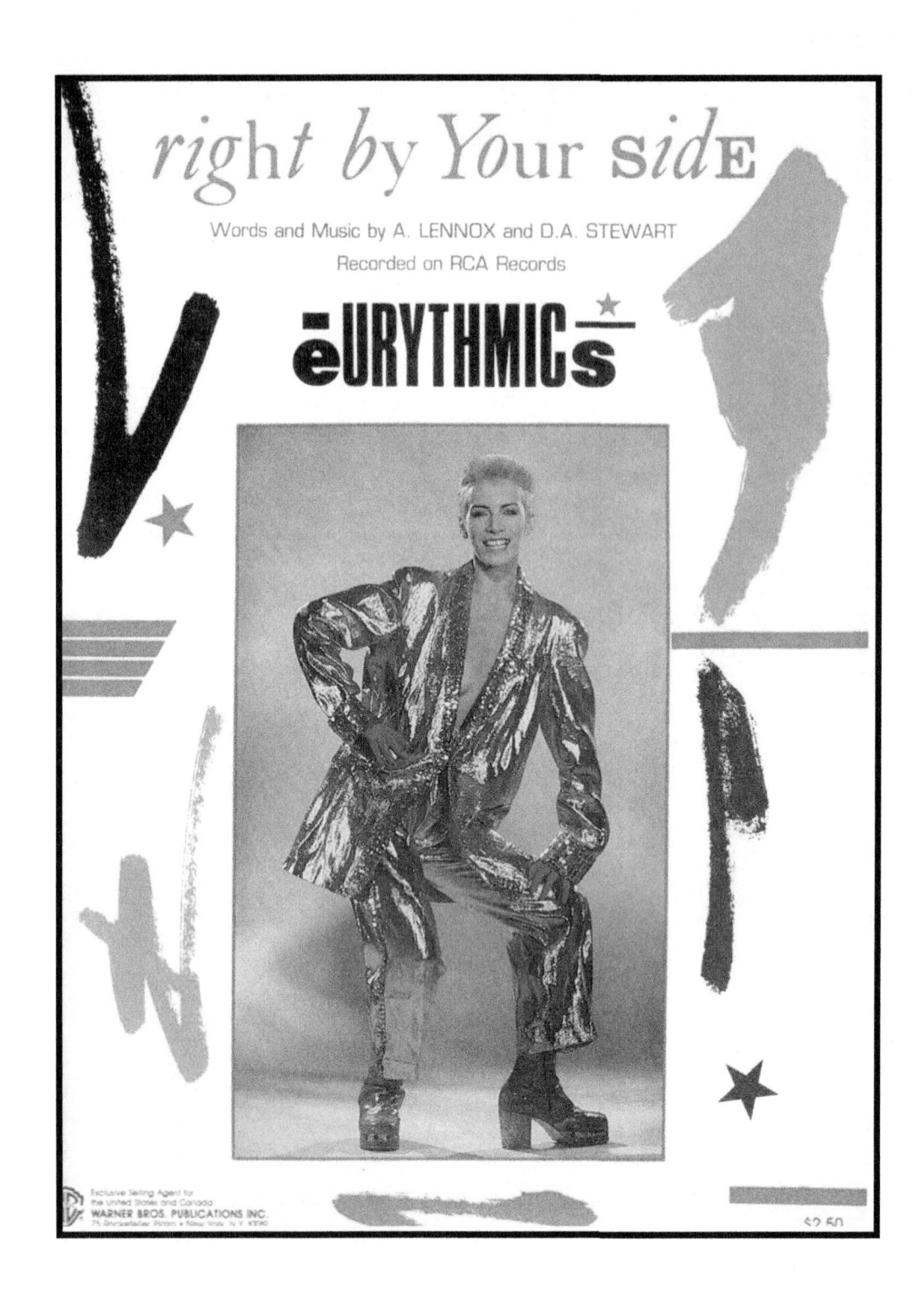

right by Your sidE

Words and Music by A. LENNOX and D.A. STEWART
Recorded on RCA Records

EURYTHMICs

USA
21.07.84: 67-49-44-40-35-33-31-**29**-44-56-69-98

Zimbabwe
17.03.84: peaked at no.**3**, charted for 14 weeks

Composed by Annie and Dave Stewart for their album *TOUCH*, *Right By Your Side* was released as the follow-up to *Who's That Girl?* in most countries.

'*Right By Your Side* is probably one of the first genuinely happy tracks we've ever recorded,' said Annie. 'It's so simple that the words might almost be trite, but I feel that. I feel like just lifting up those lyrics. The real meaning of that song for me is even simpler: it's that happiness really does exist as a possibility.'

'We were getting really fed up with ourselves being so down,' Dave observed. 'It came out sounding like calypso and at the time we really were right by each other's side.'

Right By Your Side achieved no.3 in Zimbabwe, no.9 in New Zealand, no.10 in the UK, no.13 in Sweden, no.15 in Australia and Ireland, no.29 in the USA and no.31 in Belgium.

COSMOPOLITAN

October 1984 • 75p

No sex please – I'm having a break

Win hunks of gold

What makes a lady a witch?

News! Why women prefer <u>not</u> to be boss

Sing with Victoria W Jump with Julie W

Annie Lennox goes straight

Second Wives – look after number one!

Grrrr! Meet the new Barbarians

Fiction
Erica Jong
Angela Carter
Alice Walker

9 ~ Here Comes The Rain Again by Eurythmics

UK: PB 68141 / DA 5 (1984).
  B-side: *Paint A Rumour*.

21.01.84: 20-11-**8**-10-18-29-40-61-x-89

Australia
19.03.84: peaked at no.**16**, charted for 14 weeks

Belgium
4.02.84: 38-28-**15**-16-20-22

Canada
5.03.84: peaked at no.**7**, charted for 13 weeks

Germany
20.02.84: 37-26-20-17-19-**14**-26-25-33-32-35-43-43-54

Ireland
29.01.84: 20-**8**-**8**-11-26

Netherlands
11.02.84: **33**-44-46-42-41-44

New Zealand
22.04.84: **32**-32-46-47-49

Norway
18.02.84: **10**

Sweden
20.03.84: **20** (bi-weekly)

Switzerland
18.03.84: 22-**19**-23-25-29

USA
28.01.84: 53-39-28-24-15-11-8-8-5-**4-4**-7-9-18-38-57-68-74-92-97

Zimbabwe
9.06.84: peaked at no.**15**, charted for 4 weeks

Here Comes The Rain Again was written by Annie and Dave Stewart ~ the title was inspired by an argument between the pair, following which Annie sat gazing out of a window, and seeing it was starting to rain commented, 'Here comes the rain again'.

'The whole song was about that undecided thing,' said Dave, 'like here comes depression, or here comes that downward spiral. But then it goes "so talk to me like lovers do", it's the wandering in and out of melancholy, a dark beauty that sort of is like the rose that's when it's darkest unfolding and blood red just before the garden, dies, and capturing that in kind of oblique statements and sentiments.'

Eurythmics recorded the strings for *Here Comes The Rain Again* with members of the British Philharmonic Orchestra, with Michael Kamen conducting.

'My favourite track (on *TOUCH*) is *Here Comes The Rain Again*,' said Dave. 'I'm more drawn to actual songs than weird sounds and that's why I like singles so much, because you've only got a certain amount of time to do everything.'

Released as the lead single from *TOUCH* in North America, *Here Comes The Rain Again* rose to no.4 in the Hot 100 in the United States, and peaked at no.7 in Canada.

Elsewhere, *Here Comes The Rain Again* was issued as the third single from the album, and charted at no.8 in Ireland and the UK, no.10 in Norway, no.14 in Germany, no.15 in Belgium and Zimbabwe, no.16 in Australia, no.19 in Switzerland, no.20 in Sweden, no.32 in New Zealand and no.33 in the Netherlands.

10 ~ Sexcrime (Nineteen Eighty-Four) by Eurythmics

UK: Virgin 728 (1984).
  B-side: *I Did It Just The Same*.

3.11.84: 62-44-24-7-6-**4**-9-17-17-17-22-47-72-x-94-96

Australia
24.12.84: peaked at no.**5**, charted for 18 weeks

Belgium
24.11.84: 15-10-8-5-**3**-7-10-10-15-23-31

Canada
24.12.84: peaked at no.**32**, charted for 12 weeks

France
26.01.85: 38-33-24-17-12-9-9-**7**-8-11-11-17-13-21-19-27-42-46-46

Germany
3.12.84: 63-14-7-**3**-**3**-5-5-5-8-13-15-22-38-53-60-62

Ireland
18.11.84: 30-23-**4**-5-6-11-27

Netherlands
17.11.84: 38-16-15-**12**-13-13-18-20-19-20-20-28-40

SEXCRIME
(nineteen eighty · four)

TAKEN FROM THE MOTION PICTURE SOUND TRACK ALBUM: **1984**

1984

Written and Recorded on RCA Records by

EURYTHM!CS

Exclusive Selling Agent for
the United States and Canada
WARNER BROS. PUBLICATIONS INC.

$2.50

New Zealand
27.01.85: 39-40-43-x-33-35-16-10-9-**8**-17-17-11-31-40-48-44-45

Norway
2.02.85: **9**

Sweden
21.12.84: 19-13-5-**3**-4-12 (bi-weekly)

Switzerland
16.12.84: 24-21-14-7-**6**-**6**-9-12-16-19-28-30

USA
24.11.84: 86-**81**-84-98

Sexcrime (Nineteen Eighty-Four) was written and recorded by Annie and Dave Stewart for the Eurythmics album, *SEXCRIME (FOR THE LOVE OF BIG BROTHER)*, which was the soundtrack to the film, *1984*. The film was an adaptation of George Orwell's popular 1949 novel with the same title.

Originally, *Sexcrime (Nineteen Eighty-Four)* was scheduled to feature in the film, but it was ultimately dropped, and used as background music to the film's trailer instead.

'They agreed to give us the film to put in our video and then I was really confused,' said Dave Stewart. 'I thought, "Hello, the director doesn't want to put our music in his film, but he wants to put his film in our video, in order to sell the film". And at that point we just stopped talking to them.'

Sexcrime (Nineteen Eighty-Four) gave Eurythmics one of their biggest hits in several countries, charting at no.3 in Belgium, Germany and Sweden, no.4 in Ireland and the UK, no.5 in Australia, no.6 in Switzerland, no.7 in France, no.8 in New Zealand, no.9 in Norway, no.12 in the Netherlands and no.3 in Canada.

The word 'sexcrime' in the song's title, taken from Orwell's novel where he used it as one of a number of Newspeak words, proved controversial in the United States. As a result, the single enjoyed very little exposure on MTV and other media outlets, due to its perceived 'objectionable content'. As a result, it was only a minor no.81 hit on the Hot 100.

'Do They Know It's Christmas?' by Band Aid

UK: Mercury/Phonogram FEED 1 (1984).

Here's one that got away ...

'Do They Know It's Christmas?' was composed by Bob Geldof and Midge Ure, in response to harrowing TV reports of famine in Ethiopia. The song was recorded as a charity single by numerous well known artists, including Bananarama, Bono, Boy George, Phil Collins, Duran Duran, Kool & The Gang, George Michael, Spandau Ballet, Status Quo, Sting and Paul Weller.

The original sleeve credited Annie Lennox, as she was scheduled to join Big Country, David Bowie, Holly Johnson and Paul McCartney, to record a spoken message for the B-side of the single. However, illness meant Annie wasn't able to complete her contribution in time, and so she missed out on being included.

'Do They Know It's Christmas?' topped the UK chart for five weeks, and sold a million plus copies in the first week alone. It went on the outsell *Mull Of Kintyre* by Wings, and become the UK's no.1 best-selling single of all-time ~ a title it held until 1997, when Elton John's *Candle In The Wind 1997*, a tribute to the late Diana, Princess of Wales, outsold it. To date, *'Do They Know It's Christmas?'* has sold around 3.8 million copies in the UK.

'Do They Know It's Christmas?' went to no.1 in numerous other countries, including Australia, Austria, Belgium, Canada, Denmark, Germany, Ireland, Italy, Netherlands, New Zealand, Norway, Sweden and Switzerland.

11 ~ *Julia* by Eurythmics

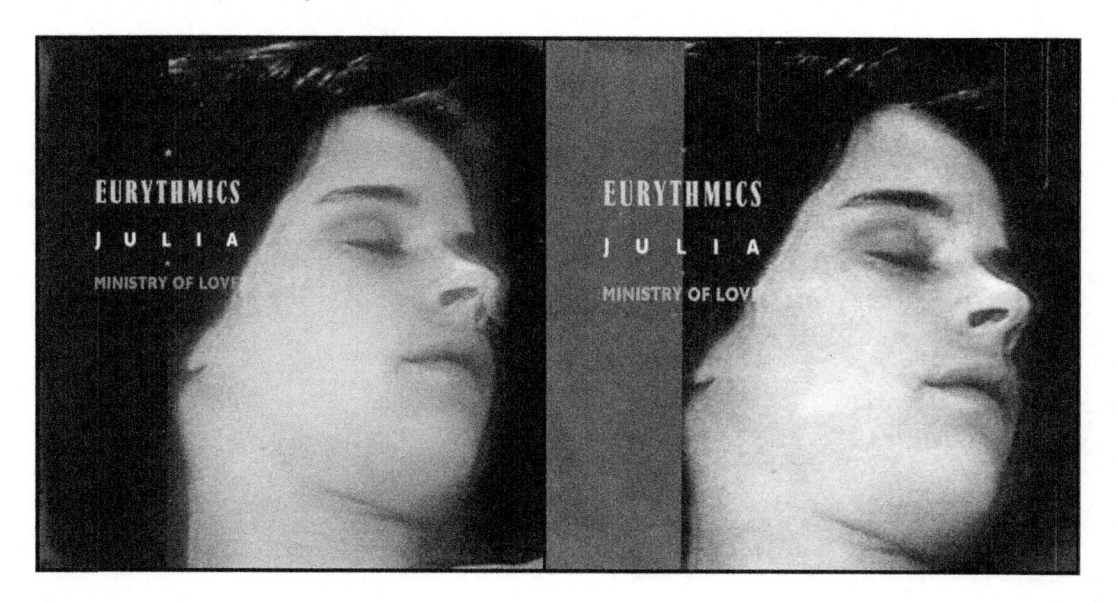

UK: Virgin VS 734 (1984).
 B-side: *Ministry Of Love*.

19.01.85: 54-**44**-47-53

Ireland
19.01.85: **17**-19

Written by Annie and Dave Stewart, *Julia* was the second and last single released from the Eurythmics album, *1984 (FOR THE LOVE OF BIG BROTHER)*. A ballad, *Julia* was played over the film's end credits.
 The single's sleeve design featured a photograph of actress Suzanna Hamilton, who played Julia, taken from the film.
 Julia proved less popular than previous Eurythmics singles, and only achieved Top 40 status in one country, Ireland, where it rose to no.17. The single charted at no.44 in the UK, but it wasn't a hit anywhere else.

12 ~ Would I Lie To You? by Eurythmics

UK: RCA 40101 (1985).
  B-side: *Here Comes That Sinking Feeling*.

20.04.85: 45-31-25-**17**-18-25-41-62-x-90

Australia
13.05.85: peaked at no.**1** (2), charted for 21 weeks

Belgium
4.05.85: 35-32-31-17-**10**-13-13-33

Canada
1.07.85: peaked at no.**3**, charted for 17 weeks

France
22.06.85: **41**-49-49

Germany
27.05.85: 53-49-41-**34**-35-46-60-57

Ireland
5.05.85: 30-15-**10**-15

Netherlands
11.05.85: 42-34-30-**24**-29-34-42-49

New Zealand
9.06.85: 33-25-17-9-7-**5**-7-8-12-14-22-32-29-32-31

Sweden
3.05.85: 12-**10-10**-17 (bi-weekly)

Switzerland
26.05.85: 29-23-27-25-**21**

USA
27.04.85: 62-46-40-36-31-26-20-16-14-8-6-**5**-10-18-28-43-66-83-98

Would I Lie To You? was composed by Annie and Dave Stewart, and was recorded for the 1985 Eurythmics album, *BE YOURSELF TONIGHT* ~ it was chosen as the album's lead single.

The accompanying music video, like the lyrics, focused on Annie confronting her cheating boyfriend, played by actor Steven Bauer, before she leaves him. The promo was directed by Mary Lambert.

Would I Lie To You? proved especially popular in Australia, where it went all the way to no.1. Elsewhere, the single achieved no.3 in Canada, no.5 in New Zealand and the United States, no.10 in Belgium, Ireland and Sweden, no.17 in the UK, no.21 in Switzerland, no.24 in the Netherlands, no.34 in Germany and no.41 in France.

13 ~ There Must Be An Angel (Playing With My Heart) by Eurythmics

UK: RCA PB 40247 (1985).
 B-side: *Grown Up Girls*.

6.07.85: 37-10-3-**1**-2-2-6-9-14-25-32-53-65

Australia
29.07.85: peaked at no.**3**, charted for 17 weeks

Austria
1.09.85: 21-**9**-13-20-23 (bi-weekly)

Belgium
3.08.85: 30-29-19-14-11-**7**-11-13-16-35

Canada
28.10.85: peaked at no.**8**, charted for 19 weeks

Finland
08.85: peaked at no.**2**, charted for 8 weeks (monthly)

France
19.10.85: 18-18-12-9-9-**8**-**8**-**8**-11-13-15-17-24-30-49

Germany
12.08.85: 58-12-8-6-**4**-**4**-6-9-16-19-28-46-54-70

Ireland
21.07.85: 5-2-**1**-4-7-11-27

Netherlands
3.08.85: 18-7-5-**3**-4-5-7-8-10-16-20-34

New Zealand
18.08.85: 31-21-6-**5**-6-8-6-9-12-16-26-44

Norway
3.08.85: 8-6-2-2-**1**-2-3-5-7

South Africa
5.10.85: peaked at no.**6**, charted for 13 weeks

Spain
14.10.85: peaked at no.**2**, charted for 25 weeks

Sweden
12.07.85: 12-3-**2**-**2**-6-15-16 (bi-weekly)

USA
3.08.85: 64-48-38-32-27-26-24-**22**-33-57-80

Zimbabwe
26.10.85: peaked at no.**5**, charted for 10 weeks

There Must Be An Angel (Playing With My Heart) was written by Annie and Dave Stewart, and was recorded by Eurythmics for their album, *BE YOURSELF TONIGHT*. The recording featured a harmonica solo by Stevie Wonder.

'We'd booked a studio in L.A. to record *There Must Be An Angel (Playing With My Heart),*' said Annie, 'and rumour had it that Stevie Wonder didn't really know what time it is, and we'd have to wait and see if he would turn up. It was getting very late and we were getting pessimistic whether he'd even turn up at all. Finally, he showed up, and he really was an adorable person … The man is a supreme musician, worth waiting for.'

Annie and Dave dedicated *There Must Be An Angel (Playing With My Heart)* to: 'Mr Stevie Wonder with love and thanks'.

The track was released as the second single from the album, and gave Annie and Dave their biggest hit in many countries, including the UK where it gave the duo their first and to date only no.1.

There Must Be An Angel (Playing With My Heart) also hit no.1 in Ireland and Norway, and achieved no.2 in Finland, Spain and Sweden, no.3 in Australia and the Netherlands, no.4 in Germany, no.5 in New Zealand and Zimbabwe, no.6 in South Africa, no.7 in Belgium, no.8 in Canada and France, no.9 in Austria and no.22 in the USA.

The German girl band No Angels recorded a cover of *There Must Be An Angel* in 2001, which went straight to no.1 in their homeland. Their version of the song also topped the chart in Austria, and peaked at no.2 in Switzerland.

14 ~ Sisters Are Doin' It For Themselves by Eurythmics And Aretha Franklin

UK: RCA PB 40339 (1985).
B-side: *I Love You Like A Ball And Chain*.

2.11.85: 38-18-10-**9**-14-18-29-37-49-51-61-x-87

Australia
18.11.85: peaked at no.**15**, charted for 15 weeks

Belgium
16.11.85: 40-**28**-31-34

Canada
9.12.85: peaked at no.**39**, charted for 3 weeks

Finland
12.85: peaked at no.**17**, charted for 4 weeks (monthly)

Germany
18.11.85: 42-31-29-**22**-25-35-35-38-46-56-58-74-71

Ireland
17.11.85: 16-**5**-6-22

SISTERS ARE DOIN' IT FOR THEMSELVES

Words and Music by **A. LENNOX** and **D.A. STEWART**
Recorded on **RCA** Records

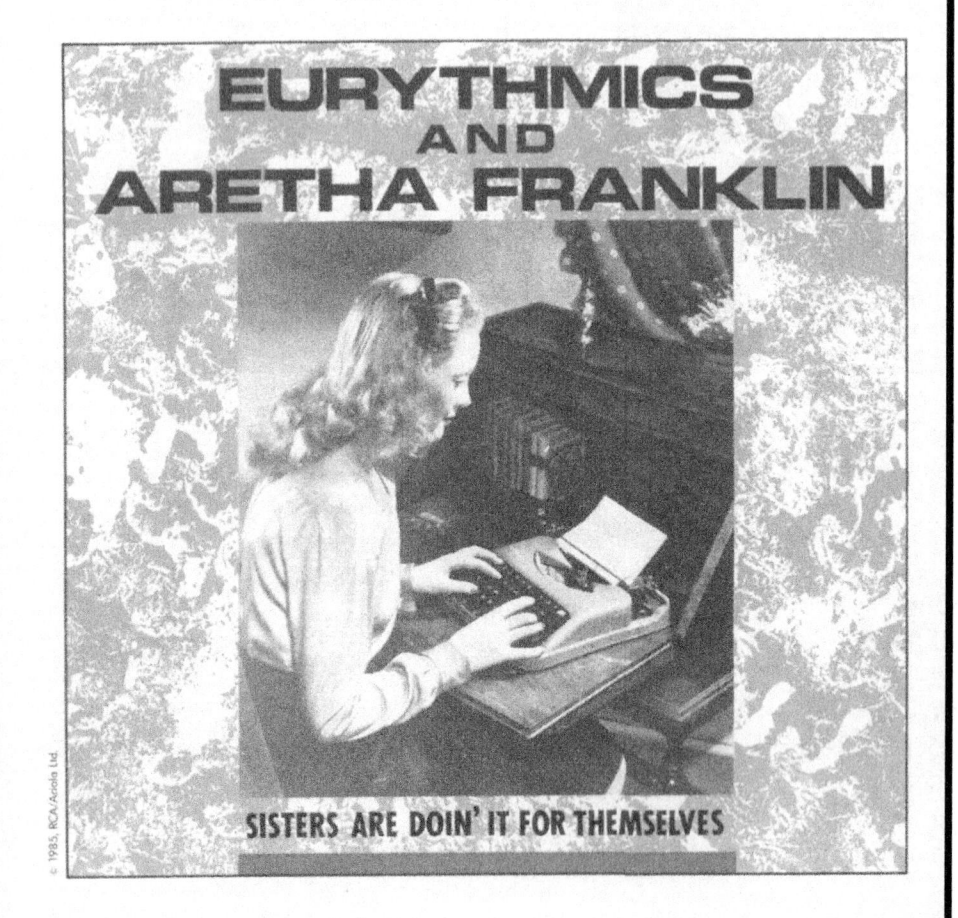

Netherlands
9.11.85: 46-**17**-21-27-25-44

New Zealand
15.12.85: 15-15-15-15-15-**6**-7-9-17-27-37-45

Switzerland
22.12.85: 28-23-**20**-26-29-28

USA
19.10.85: 62-45-39-37-31-26-24-**18**-24-37-42-51-60-70-82

Zimbabwe
1.02.86: peaked at no.**15**, charted for 6 weeks

Sisters Are Doin' It for Themselves was written by Annie and Dave Stewart, and was recorded by Eurythmics with Aretha Franklin. As well as featuring on the Eurythmics album *BE YOURSELF TONIGHT*, *Sisters Are Doin' It For Themselves* was also released on Aretha's 1985 album, *WHO'S ZOOMIN' WHO?*

'It was a challenge,' said Annie, 'to write a pop song that could be played on radio, yet was a feminist anthem. I woke up one morning and wrote all the words. I had a vision of it, and said to Dave that this idea needs a fantastic woman to sing it with.'

Annie's first choice was Tina Turner.

'I really love Tina Turner's voice,' she said, 'and Tina was really emerging at that period as a phoenix from the ashes out of that Ike and Tina thing. She was approached, but she felt that the statement of the song didn't really suit her image, and she declined the offer. I was very disappointed actually, because I really wanted to sing with her.'

Next, Annie and Dave approached Aretha Franklin, and after she accepted they flew to Aretha's home town, Detroit, to record the song.

'I got along with her but we didn't have an immediate rapport,' said Annie. 'Aretha struck me as rather shy, a bit sad, a bit lonely. She had an entourage which I thought was a bit eccentric, I wasn't used to it.'

Sisters Are Doin' It For Themselves was the third single released from *BE YOURSELF TONIGHT* and, while it couldn't match the success of *There Must Be An Angel (Playing With My Heart)*, it was successful in most countries, charting at no.5 in Ireland, no.6 in New Zealand, no.9 in the UK, no.15 in Australia and Zimbabwe, no.17 in Finland and the Netherlands, no.18 in the USA, no.20 in Switzerland, no.22 in Germany, no.28 in Belgium and no.39 in Canada.

Sisters Are Doin' It For Themselves picked up a Grammy nomination, for Best R&B Performance by a Duo or Group with Vocals, but Eurythmics and Aretha lost out to the Commodores, who took the award for their tribute to Jackie Wilson and Marvin Gaye, *Nightshift*.

15 ~ It's Alright (Baby's Coming Back) by Eurythmics

UK: RCA PB 40375 (1985).
  B-side: *Conditioned Soul*.

11.01.86: 39-13-**12**-14-17-33-40-54

Australia
24.02.86: peaked at no.**32**, charted for 13 weeks

Austria
1.04.86: 17-**14**-17 (bi-weekly)

Belgium
22.02.86: **26**-30-34

Canada
14.04.86: peaked at no.**35**, charted for 7 weeks

Germany
10.02.86: 29-27-27-**22**-29-34-46-59-67

Ireland
26.01.86: 25-9-**8**-27

Netherlands
25.01.86: 27-**21**-22-22-24-35-48

New Zealand
16.03.86: 29-25-20-20-**18**-25-23-34

Switzerland
2.03.86: 30-**23-23**-29-28-26

USA
15.02.86: 89-85-81-**78**-84-99

Written and recorded by Annie and Dave Stewart, *It's Alright (Baby's Coming Back)* was the fourth and final single issued from the Eurythmics album, *BE YOURSELF TONIGHT*.

'We really don't understand a great deal about life after death,' said Annie. 'I feel this song embodies that unknown in a way. I was thinking about the good, gentler qualities that people have in their relationships, the things that pull us through, even though the physical body dies. It's those gentler, nobler qualities in human nature that endure. It's like a collective soul.'

This theme was explored in the music video, albeit with some rather dated animation, where Dave's soul is shown as a shadow travelling in cartoon-like cars, planes and trains.

'I do remember seeing the first cut of the video,' said Annie, 'and throwing a diva-esque tantrum, floods of tears. We had to re-shoot it. If you do something, you have to live with it. That's why we're control freaks.'

Although it didn't sell as well as the previous three singles from the album ~ by now, most Eurythmics fans had already bought the album ~ *It's Alright (Baby's Coming Back)* continued the duo's run of hits. It achieved no.8 in Ireland, no.12 in the UK, no.14 in Austria, no.18 in New Zealand, no.21 in the Netherlands, no.22 in Germany, no.23 in Switzerland and a lowly no.78 in the USA.

Annie and Dave Stewart's song-writing talents was recognised, with *It's Alright (Baby's Coming Back)* winning them the 1986 Ivor Novello Award, for Best Song Musically and Lyrically.

16 ~ When Tomorrow Comes by Eurythmics

UK: RCA DA 7 (1986).
 B-side: *Take Your Pain Away*.

14.06.86: 38-**30**-35-44-68-69-83-86-90-x-95-86

Australia
30.06.86: peaked at no.**7**, charted for 18 weeks

Belgium
21.06.86: 34-28-25-24-24-27-21-**18**-25-36

Denmark
4.07.86: 11-x-x-x-x-x-15-10-**9**-11-12-14

Finland
06.86: peaked at no.**9**, charted for 8 weeks (monthly)

Germany
7.07.86: 43-31-26-25-**22-22**-24-33-40-51-57

Ireland
25.06.86: **13**-21

Netherlands
28.06.86: 35-34-27-23-**22**-24-x-50

New Zealand
17.08.86: 37-29-35-**19**-20-25-30-40-45-50

Norway
21.06.86: 7-**5**-7-6-7-7-**5**-7-8

South Africa
7.09.86: **19**

Spain
22.09.86: peaked at no.**12**, charted for 16 weeks

Sweden
11.06.86: 19-5-**4**-5-7-19 (bi-weekly)

When Tomorrow Comes was written by Annie, Dave Stewart and keyboard player Pat Seymour, and was recorded by Eurythmics ~ with Pat Seymour on keyboards ~ for their 1986 album, *REVENGE*.

With the exception of North America, where it wasn't issued as a single, *When Tomorrow Comes* was released as the album's lead single. It proved most popular in Scandinavia and Australia, charting at no.4 in Sweden, no.5 in Norway, no.7 in Australia, no.9 in Denmark and Finland, no.12 in Spain, no.13 in Ireland, no.18 n Belgium, no.19 in New Zealand and South Africa, no.22 in Germany and the Netherlands, and a disappointing no.30 in the UK.

17 ~ Thorn In My Side by Eurythmics

UK: RCA DA 8 (1986).
  B-side: *In This Town*.

6.09.86: 29-16-10-7-**5**-7-11-17-32-44-63
10.01.87: 100

Australia
17.11.86: peaked at no.**12**, charted for 22 weeks

Austria
15.10.86: 16-18-**14-14**-18-24 (bi-weekly)

Belgium
13.09.86: **34**

Canada
9.02.87: peaked at no.**34**, charted for 8 weeks

Denmark
19.09.86: 12-13-**7**-10-11-11

Finland
09.86: peaked at no.**6**, charted for 8 weeks (monthly)

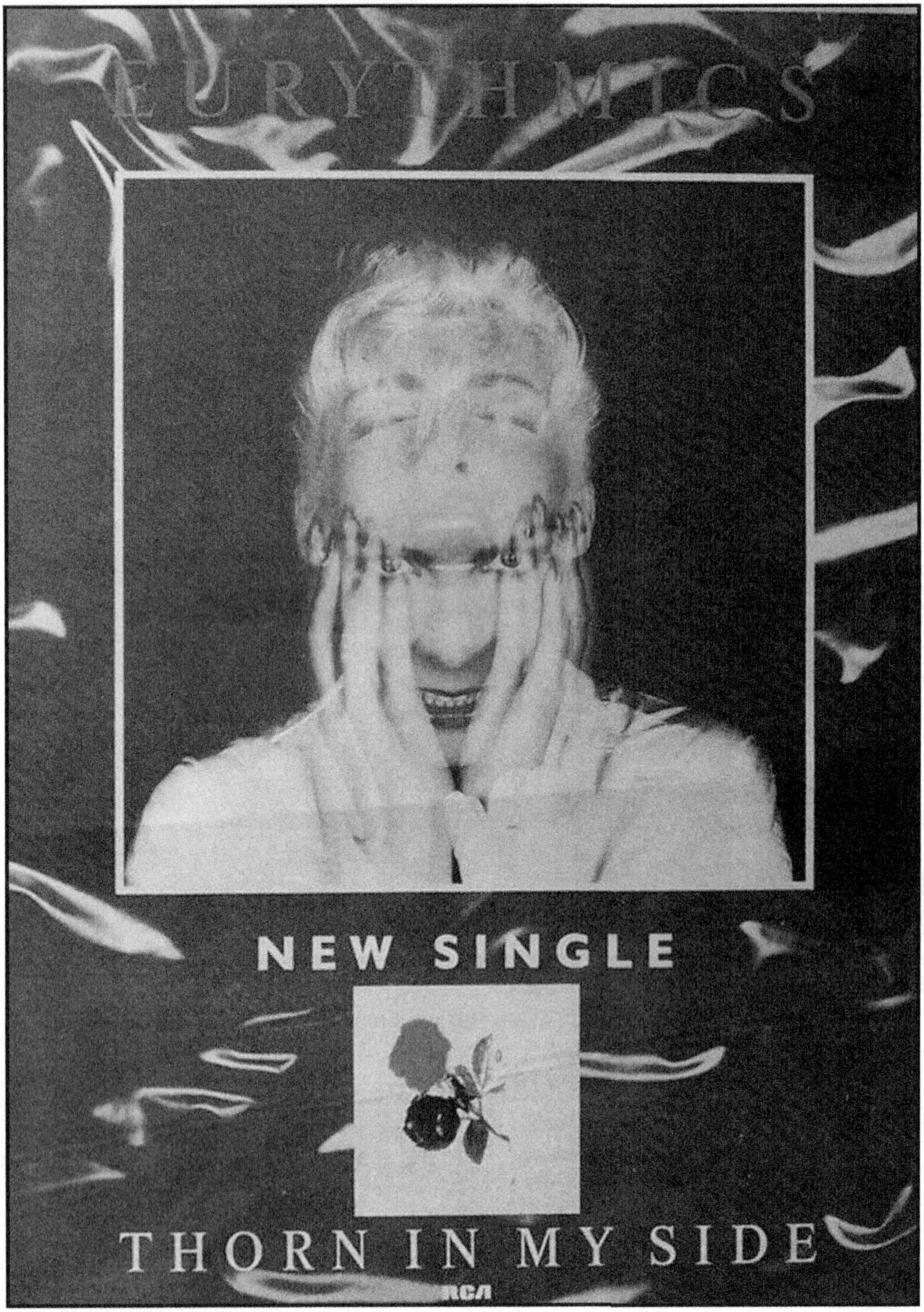
EURYTHMICS
NEW SINGLE
THORN IN MY SIDE
RCA

Germany
22.09.86: 48-40-28-**26**-29-35-42-44-48-59-60-66-71-74

Ireland
14.09.86: 16-3-**2**-7-11-16-23

New Zealand
18.01.87: 20-13-10-**7**-8-16-15-21-44

Spain
22.12.86: peaked at no.**13**, charted for 4 weeks

Sweden
10.09.86: 7-**6**-11-13 (bi-weekly)

USA
15.11.86: 94-86-75-**68-68**-78-95-95-97

Written by Annie and Dave Stewart, *Thorn In My Side* was the second single lifted from the Eurythmics album, *REVENGE*, and in several countries it out-performed the first, *When Tomorrow Comes*.

'It had been so heavy for her (Annie), and this was her release,' said Dave Stewart. 'This period was when we started to become affected by other people and bring them into our music. I can't say that we were no longer emotionally involved because being with Annie was, well, like having seven thousand emotions ~ there was never a straightforward day. You know, it doesn't have to be sexual.'

In rising to no.5, *Thorn In My Side* gave Eurythmics their ninth Top 10 single in the UK ~ however, it would prove to be the duo's last. Elsewhere, the single achieved no.2 in Ireland, no.6 in Finland and Sweden, no.7 in Denmark and New Zealand, no.12 in Australia, no.13 in Spain, no.14 in Austria, no.26 in Germany, no.34 in Belgium and Canada, and a lowly no.68 in the USA.

The music video for *Thorn In My Side*, directed by Dave Stewart and Chris Ashbrook, saw Eurythmics and their band playing before an audience that included a gang of Hell's Angels. Since he was recording and touring with Annie and Dave at the time, the promo featured an appearance by Blondie's drummer, Clem Burke.

18 ~ Missionary Man by Eurythmics

UK: RCA DA 10 (1987).
  B-side: *The Last Time (Live Version)*.

28.02.87: **31-31**-40-63

Australia
8.09.86: peaked at no.**9**, charted for 13 weeks

Belgium
11.04.87: **34**

Canada
29.09.86: peaked at no.**7**, charted for 14 weeks

Ireland
1.03.87: 27-**13**-16

Netherlands
21.03.87: **77**

New Zealand
19.10.86: 47-36-15-33-24-x-14-**12**-19-17-17-17-25-28-25-29-37-32-49

USA
26.07.86: 81-76-62-57-45-34-28-23-18-16-15-**14**-18-33-62-92

Missionary Man was written by Annie and Dave Stewart, and was partly inspired by Annie's relationship with Radha Raman, a Hare Krishna devotee to whom she was briefly married, from 1984-85.

'Obviously, there is a personal meaning in *Missionary Man* for me,' she said, 'because of my past history, but I also think that there are a great deal of people in the media, in the form of politicians or religious speakers or philosophical people, people who are generally trying to have some power over other people, who I just don't trust.'

Another influence was a friend of Dave Stewart's, Bob Dylan, whom he and Annie visited at his home.

'Annie was there and we were all drunk on tequila,' said Dave. 'Dylan was reciting the lyrics to these songs as the backing tracks were playing, but he was just making them up on the spot, and Annie was trying to scribble them all down as he went along.'

Back home, Annie created a poem from her scribblings, which eventually progressed into the lyrics for *Missionary Man*.

In North America, *Missionary Man* was released as the lead single from *REVENGE*, and achieved no.7 in Canada and no.14 in the United States, where the song also went to no.1 on Billboard's Mainstream Rock Tracks chart.

In Australasia and Japan, *Missionary Man* was the second single lifted from *REVENGE*, and it charted at no.9 in Australia and no.12 in New Zealand.

Missionary Man was less successful in Europe, where it was issued as the fourth and final single from *REVENGE*. It achieved no.13 in Ireland, no.31 in the UK and no.34 in Belgium, but failed to chart in many countries.

Annie and Dave won a Grammy Award for *Missionary Man*, for Best Rock Performance by a Duo or Group with Vocals.

19 ~ The Miracle Of Love by Eurythmics

UK: RCA DA 9 (1986).
   B-side: *When Tomorrow Comes (Live Version)*.

29.11.86: 38-29-29-28-25-**23**-25-43-75-87-x-98

Australia
9.02.87: peaked at no.**14**, charted for 14 weeks

Belgium
22.11.86: 34-32-22-**18**-31

France
13.12.86: 45-32-36-32-33-24-21-17-19-**16**-19-27-38-46

Germany
26.01.87: 58-70-54-**53**-58-74

Ireland
7.12.86: **10**-13

Netherlands
29.11.86: **43**

New Zealand
8.03.87: **30**-32-31-35-41

Spain
9.02.87: peaked at no.**2**, charted for 11 weeks

Sweden
17.12.86: **18** (bi-weekly)

Switzerland
30.11.86: 24-26-27-**21**-22-27-24-29-x-26

Written by Annie and Dave Stewart, *The Miracle Of Love* was released as the third single from the Eurythmics album *REVENGE* in most countries.
 'We both wanted to meet somebody else,' said Dave, 'you now, "Let's go, I want to fall in love!". That's how we both felt. We both wanted to meet someone solid. We wanted that for each other, we didn't want it to be fucked up all the time.'
 The Miracle Of Love was a modest hit, charting at no.2 in Spain, no.10 in Ireland, no.14 in Australia, no.16 in France, no.18 in Belgium and Sweden, no.21 in Switzerland, no.23 in the UK, no.30 in New Zealand, no.43 in the Netherlands and no.53 in Germany.
 The Miracle Of Love wasn't issued as a single in North America.

20 ~ Beethoven (I Love To Listen To) by Eurythmics

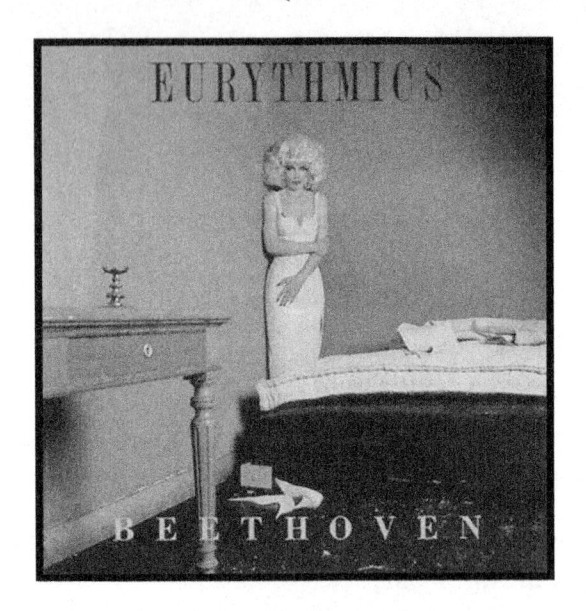

UK: RCA DA 11 (1987).
B-side: *Heaven*.

24.10.87: 30-**25**-31-41-63

Australia
2.11.87: peaked at no.**13**, charted for 15 weeks

Belgium
24.10.87: 40-33-36-30-**28**-34-34

Denmark
23.10.87: 9-7-6-**4**-11

Finland
11.87: peaked at no.**15**, charted for 4 weeks (monthly)

Germany
9.11.87: 42-42-32-**28-28**-39-52-52-59-75

Ireland
25.10.87: **11**-13

Netherlands
31.10.87: 97-93-82-63-52-43-**41**-52-77

New Zealand
20.12.87: 13-13-13-13-8-7-**6**-10-15-17-23-37-33-50

Norway
31.10.87: 9-8-**6**-8

Spain
16.11.87: peaked at no.**18**, charted for 9 weeks

Sweden
28.10.87: **9**-17 (bi-weekly)

Switzerland
8.11.87: 27-**19**-20-25-24

Beethoven (I Love To Listen To) was written by Annie and Dave Stewart, who recorded the track for the seventh Eurythmics album, *SAVAGE*, released in 1987.

'It was like an abstract painting,' said Annie. 'The whole thing is very symbolic, using that line "I love to listen to Beethoven" was just something I wrote down one day, and for me it's a symbol for when people feel really bad and they listen to classical music ... The song itself is like going into a person's head and seeing all these fractured thoughts and emotions, and everything being torn apart.'

Chosen as the lead single in most countries, *Beethoven (I Love To Listen To)* was another modest hit, and achieved no.4 in Denmark, no.6 in New Zealand and Norway, no.9 in Sweden, no.11 in Ireland, no.13 in Australia, no.15 in Finland, no.18 in Spain, no.19 in Switzerland, no.25 in the UK, no.28 in Belgium and Germany, and no.41 in the Netherlands.

Although it was passed over for single release in North America, *Beethoven (I Love To Listen To)* was listed alongside *I Need A Man*, when the latter was issued as a 12" single.

Annie and Dave shot music videos for every track on their *SAVAGE album*, all directed by Sophie Muller. In the promo for *Beethoven (I Love To Listen To)*, Annie played a woman with split personalities: a dowdy housewife, seen knitting in her spotless house, who transforms into a sexy blonde who trashes her spotless house.

21 ~ Shame by Eurythmics

UK: RCA DA 14 (1987).
B-side: *I've Got A Lover (Back In Japan)*.

19.12.87: 76-58-63-47-43-**41**-62

Australia
8.02.88: peaked at no.**39**, charted for 8 weeks

Belgium
30.01.88: **37**

Germany
25.01.88: 57-**53**-56-67-69

Netherlands
9.01.88: 84-58-**44**-54-76

New Zealand
20.03.88: **23**-35-30-30-33-48-32

South Africa
26.05.88: peaked at no.**16**, charted for 6 weeks

Spain
25.01.88: peaked at no.**26**, charted for 8 weeks

Shame was written by Annie and Dave Stewart, and name-checked the Beatles and Rolling Stones. It was the second single lifted from the duo's *SAVAGE* album in most countries ~ however, like *Beethoven (I Love To Listen To)*, it was passed over for single release in North America.

Chart-wise, *Shame* struggled in most countries, peaking at no.16 in South Africa, no.23 in New Zealand, no.26 in Spain, no.37 in Belgium, no.39 in Australia, no.41 in the UK, no.44 in the Netherlands and no.53 in Germany.

22 ~ I Need A Man by Eurythmics

UK: RCA DA 15 (1987).
  B-side: *I Need You.*

9.04.88: 31-**26**-28-42-73

Australia
16.05.88: peaked at no.**78**, charted for 6 weeks

Belgium
11.06.88: **35**

Canada
8.02.88: peaked at no.**14**, charted for 15 weeks

Ireland
17.04.87: **23**-24

New Zealand
22.05.88: **19**-34-30-27

USA
19.12.87: 87-70-70-67-55-51-**46**-54-72-95

I Need A Man was written by Annie and Dave Stewart, who recorded the song for the Eurythmics album, *SAVAGE*.

In North America, *I Need A Man* was released as the lead single from the album, charting at no.14 in Canada and no.46 in the United States. The 12" single was promoted as a double A-side with *Beethoven (I Love To Listen To)*, and rose to no.6 on Billboard's Hot Dance Club Play chart.

In most other countries, *I Need A Man* was the third single lifted from *SAVAGE*, and was only a modest hit. It achieved no.19 in New Zealand, no.23 in Ireland, no.26 in the UK and no.35 in Belgium.

The music video, directed by Sophie Muller, saw Annie in the same sexy blonde persona she's transformed into during the *Beethoven (I Love To Listen To)* promo, singing *I Need A Man* in a nightclub setting.

23 ~ You Have Placed A Chill In My Heart by Eurythmics

UK: RCA DA 16 (1988).
  B-side: *You Have Placed A Chill In My Heart (Acoustic Version)*.

11.06.88: 37-25-18-**16**-19-33-51-73-x-91

Ireland
26.06.88: 19-**15**-27

New Zealand
25.09.88: 35-40-**31**-43-45-x-x-32-46-46-47

USA
28.05.88: 95-78-73-65-**64**-67-86

You Have Placed A Chill In My Heart was composed by Annie and Dave Stewart, and was recorded by Eurythmics for the album, *SAVAGE*.
    The track was released as the second single from the album in North America, and as the fourth and final single in most other countries. It became the only single from the album to achieve Top 20 status in the UK, where it rose to no.16. Elsewhere, *You Have Placed A Chill In My Heart* charted at no.15 in Ireland, no.31 in New Zealand and no.64 in the USA, but it wasn't a hit in most countries.

24 ~ Put A Little Love In Your Heart

UK: A&M 484 (1988).
B-side: *A Great Big Piece Of Love* (The Spheres Of Celestial Influence).

12.11.88: 93-78-80-71-45-38-32-**28**-35-57-72

Australia
12.12.88: peaked at no.**8**, charted for 17 weeks

Austria
1.02.89: 9-**4**-6-9-11-17-27-29 (bi-weekly)

Belgium
10.12.88: 31-20-20-18-15-14-**13**-20-30-40

Canada
6.02.89: peaked at no.**7**, charted for 14 weeks

Germany
16.01.89: 27-24-**20**-**20**-21-**20**-30-35-49-58-68

Ireland
11.12.88: **30**

Netherlands
26.11.88: 90-38-17-14-10-**9**-13-24-46-61-88

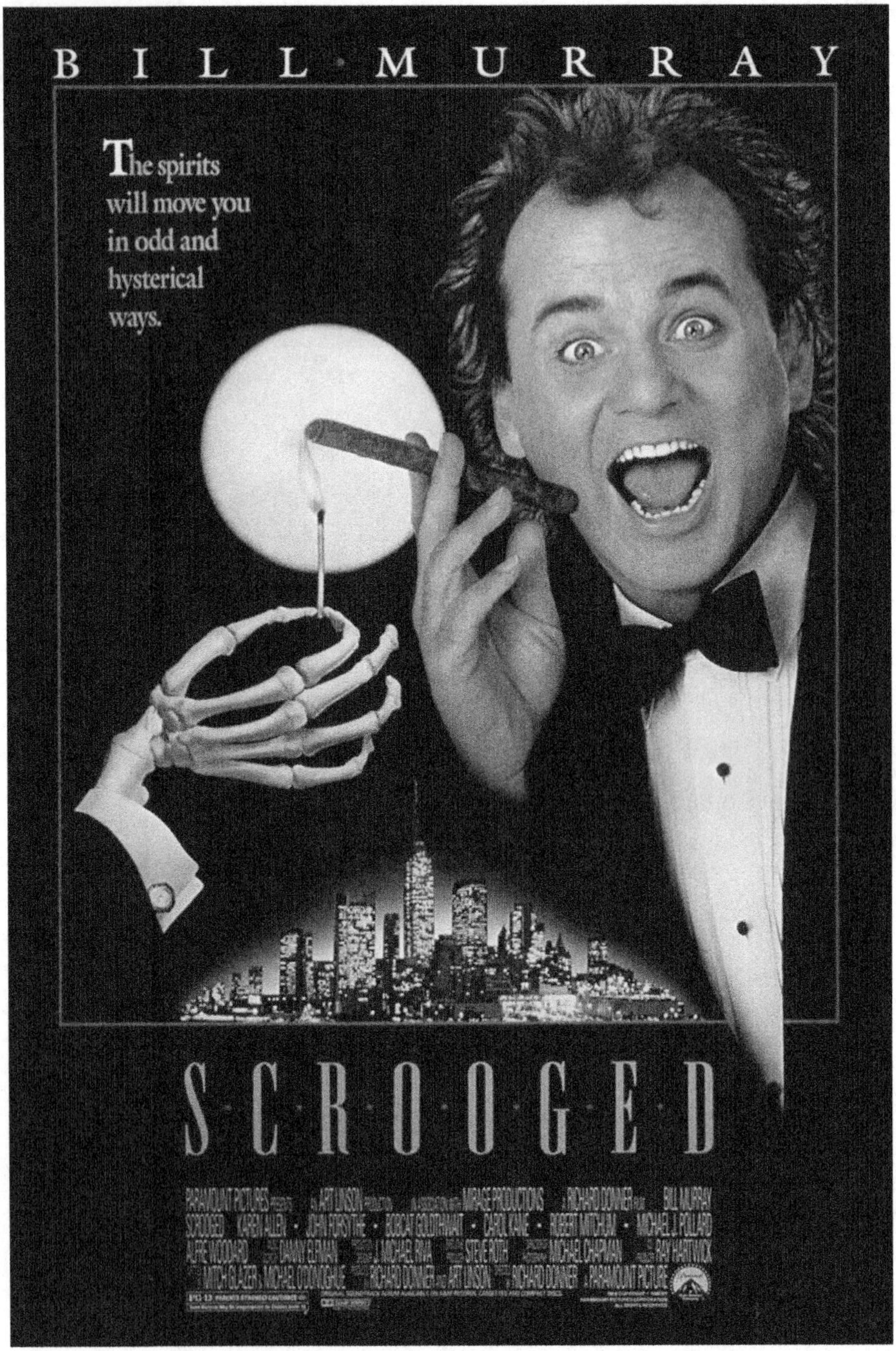
BILL MURRAY
The spirits will move you in odd and hysterical ways.
SCROOGED
PARAMOUNT PICTURES
ART LINSON
MIRAGE PRODUCTIONS
RICHARD DONNER
BILL MURRAY
SCROOGED KAREN ALLEN • JOHN FORSYTHE • BOBCAT GOLDTHWAIT • CAROL KANE • ROBERT MITCHUM • MICHAEL J. POLLARD
ALFRE WOODARD DANNY ELFMAN J. MICHAEL RIVA STEVE ROTH MICHAEL CHAPMAN RAY HARTWICK
MITCH GLAZER MICHAEL O'DONOGHUE RICHARD DONNER ART LINSON RICHARD DONNER A PARAMOUNT PICTURE
PG-13

New Zealand
18.12.88: 33-33-33-33-**7**-**7**-11-9-18-16-14-31-24-36-48-48

Switzerland
15.01.89: 22-**11**-16-14-14-17-22-29-30

USA
5.11.88: 96-71-53-42-34-29-23-19-19-12-**9**-10-17-33-46-72-96

Put A Little Love In Your Heart was composed by Jackie DeShannon, her brother Randy Myers and Jimmy Holiday, and was originally recorded by DeShannon in 1969 ~ she took the song to no.4 on the Hot 100 in the United States, and to no.12 in Canada.

Annie recorded a cover of *Put A Little Love In Your Heart* as a duet with Al Green, for the 1988 film, *Scrooged*, a festive comedy that starred Bill Murray and Karen Allen. It was the first single Annie released that saw her credited her under her own name. The duet was produced by Dave Stewart.

Annie and Al Green took their version of *Put A Little Love In Your Heart* to no.4 in Austria, no.7 in Canada and New Zealand, no.8 in Australia, no.9 in the Netherlands and USA, no.11 in Switzerland, no.13 in Belgium, no.20 in Germany, no.28 in the UK and no.30 in Ireland.

25 ~ Revival by Eurythmics

UK: RCA DA 17 (1989).
 B-side: *Precious*.

26.08.89: 40-30-**26**-31-41-59

Australia
24.09.89: 38-19-20-18-**14**-18-22-28-37-43

Belgium
2.09.89: 47-41-36-31-**19**-33-40-33-36

Denmark
18.08.89: 14-7-**5**-7-9-15

Finland
09.89: peaked at no.**16**, charted for 4 weeks (monthly)

France
28.10.89: **46**-47

Germany
19.09.89: 59-56-**33**-37-36-38-56-62-76-73-89-83-94-96

Ireland
27.08.89: **14**-20-27-27

Netherlands
26.08.89: 78-57-35-27-**25**-29-35-46-72-90

New Zealand
8.10.89: 38-31-31-42-34-**21**-48

Sweden
23.08.89: 16-**7**-11-19 (bi-weekly)

Switzerland
10.09.89: 21-15-10-9-**8**-10-13-20-23-22

Annie and Dave Stewart co-wrote *Revival* with keyboard player Patrick Seymour and Charlie Wilson of The Gap Band, who also contributed backing vocals when Eurythmics recorded the track for their 1989 album, *WE TOO ARE ONE*.

'We were recording in one room,' said Dave, 'and Charlie Wilson and our keyboard player Patrick Seymour were messing around, just playing on their own. Charlie was singing something. It was actually just "la-*LA*", but we thought it was "Re-vi-Val". At least that's what it sounded like. So, Annie said, "Oh, yeah ~ Revival!" and we all started messing around with it. Within fifteen minutes it was a song. We were all clapping our hands with glee.'

Revival wasn't released as a single in North America, but was chosen as the album's lead single in most other countries. It charted at no.5 in Denmark, no.7 in Sweden, no.8 in Switzerland, no.14 in Australia and Ireland, no.16 in Finland, no.19 in Belgium, no.21 in New Zealand, no.25 in the Netherlands, no.26 in the UK, no.33 in Germany and no.46 in France.

26 ~ Don't Ask Me Why by Eurythmics

UK: RCA DA 19 (1989).
  B-side: *Rich Girl*.

4.11.89: 44-29-**25**-28-38-64-x-x-88-99

Australia
10.12.89: 46-50-47-**35**-41

Belgium
23.12.89: **31**

Canada
18.12.89: peaked at no.**13**, charted for 15 weeks

Germany
18.12.89: 68-75-75-**56**-59-57-59-**56**-62-80-84-99-92

Ireland
12.11.89: 29-**17**

Netherlands
11.11.89: 85-61-52-49-**45**-68-91

Switzerland
3.12.89: **30**

EURYTHMICS DON'T ASK ME WHY

NEW SINGLE

now available as a 12" picture disc

in an individually numbered limited edition.

USA
30.09.89: 81-69-64-56-47-**40**-48-76-100

Written by Annie and Dave Stewart, *Don't Ask Me Why* was chosen as the lead single from the Eurythmics album *WE TOO ARE ONE* in North America, and was released as the follow-up to *Revival* elsewhere.

The single achieved no.13 in Canada, no.17 in Ireland, no.25 in the UK, no.30 in Switzerland, no.31 in Belgium, no.35 in Australia, no.40 in the USA, no.45 in the Netherlands and no.56 in Germany.

Don't Ask Me Why was issued as a 12" picture disc in the UK.

27 ~ The King And Queen Of America by Eurythmics

UK: RCA DA 23 (1989).
B-side: *See No Evil*.

3.02.90: 34-**29**-33-48-68

Australia
5.03.90: peaked at no.**76**, charted for 4 weeks

Belgium
17.03.90: 39-**33**-39

Germany
19.03.90: 70-68-**51**-56-57-64-59-82-74-87-85-79

Ireland
11.02.90: **23**

Netherlands
10.02.90: 85-65-56-46-40-**38**-54-77-93

The King And Queen Of America was written by Annie and Dave Stewart, and was recorded by Eurythmics for their album, *WE TOO ARE ONE*.
 'It's an angry song that stems from one of my pet hates,' said Annie, 'which is the cult of personality. In America in particular, people want to invite the media into their living rooms and show off their lives. The couple in the song are completely sold on all the

glittering icons that are supposed to mean success and the attainment of the American dream. I'm very curious about what success is, and wonder why people won't look at it more critically.'

The accompanying music video explored the song's theme further, and parodied aspects of American popular culture, with Annie and Dave playing Nancy & Ronald Reagan, Marilyn Monroe & Elvis Presley, Dale Evans & Roy Rogers, a cheerleader and an American footballer, and a game show hostess and host, amongst others.

'American radio loved the song *The King And Queen Of America* for the first ten days,' said Dave, 'and then they had all these phone calls from irate fascist Americans saying, "What the fuck are you playing that for?! They're taking the piss out of our society". And so they took it off the air. They're so conservative over there it's unbelievable.'

Not surprisingly, *The King And Queen Of America* wasn't released as a single in North America, but in most countries it was issued as the third single from *WE TOO ARE ONE*. Although not a huge success, the single charted at no.23 in Ireland, no.29 in the UK, no.33 in Belgium and no.38 in the Netherlands. The single was also a minor hit in Australia and Germany.

28 ~ Angel by Eurythmics

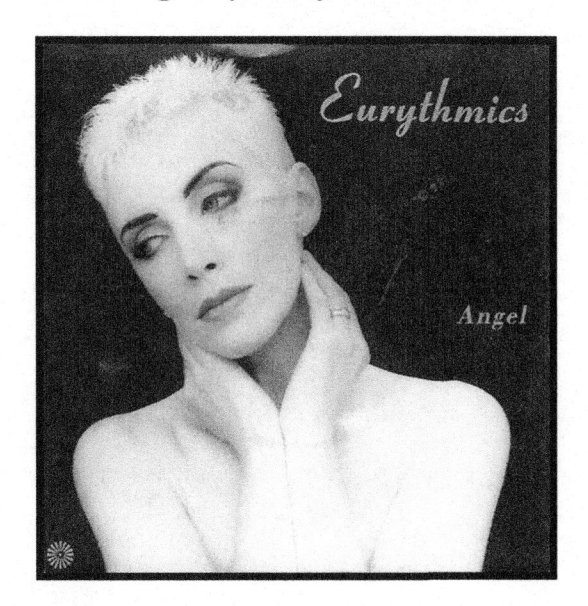

UK: RCA DA 21 (1989).
B-side: *Angel (Choir Version)*.

12.05.90: 49-27-**23**-33-45-68

Ireland
25.05.90: **25**

Angel, inspired by the death of Annie's great-aunt, was composed by Annie and Dave Stewart, and was recorded by Eurythmics for their album, *WE TOO ARE ONE*. The song is about a 57 year old woman who is dying, and instead chooses to take her own life.

'I once had written a poem about a woman who was my great-aunt,' said Annie, 'she had died ~ she was actually my first experience of death. I was eleven years old.'

Angel was released as the second single from the album in North America, and as the fourth and final single in most other countries. It turned out to be the last new Eurythmics single for almost a decade.

Annie and Dave promoted *Angel* with a music video directed by Sophie Muller, however, due to the occult nature of the promo, which featured a séance, it wasn't aired by MTV in the United States, and the single failed to enter the Hot 100 chart.

Angel fared better in the UK and Ireland, where it rose to no.23 and no.25, respectively, but the single didn't sell well enough to chart in most countries.

Annie recorded a solo version of *Angel* for the 1997 album, *DIANA, PRINCESS OF WALES – TRIBUTE*.

29 ~ Why

UK: RCA PD 75317 (1992).
  B-side: *Primitive*.

28.03.92: 9-6-**5**-11-18-39-51-70
28.03.09: 93

Australia
6.04.92: peaked at no.**17**, charted for 12 weeks

Austria
19.04.92: 22-20-21-22-16-12-17-13-**11**-20-22-22

Belgium
18.04.92: 26-24-12-6-**4**-5-7-9-15-26-47

Denmark
27.03.92: 10-**9**

Germany
6.04.92: 85-40-13-16-**12**-13-13-15-18-21-25-26-32-31-43-46-77-85-95

Ireland
30.03.92: 23-6-**5**-8-21

Netherlands
21.03.92: 70-58-46-32-24-17-13-**8**-9-15-21-27-35-58-76

New Zealand
26.04.92: 24-**15**-20-28-26-22-30-34-44

Norway
11.04.92: 8-x-x-**6**

Spain
28.03.92: peaked at no.**11**, charted for 5 weeks

Sweden
1.04.92: 14-12-**10**-12-21-37 (bi-weekly)

Switzerland
12.04.92: 27-20-15-11-9-10-**6**-9-12-11-16-13-18-24-29-25-24-24-36-36-35

USA
16.05.92: 100-87-77-64-53-46-42-41-37-**34**-38-45-56-61-69-78-90-94-98-95

Written by Annie, *Why* was chosen as the lead single from her debut solo album, *DIVA* ~ it was the first single released credited to Annie and Annie alone.

Directed by Sophie Muller, the music video for *Why* was filmed during the photo shoot for the *DIV*A album cover. It won Annie the Best Female Video at the 1992 MTV Video Music Awards.

Why got Annie's solo career off to a great start, charting at no.4 in Belgium, no.5 in Ireland and the UK, no.6 in Norway and Switzerland, no.8 in the Netherlands, no.9 in Denmark, no.10 in Sweden, no.11 in Austria and Spain, no.12 in Germany, no.15 in New Zealand, no.17 in Australia and no.34 in the USA.

Spanish producer DJ Sammy, with vocals by Britta Medeiros, covered *Why* in 2005. His version achieved no.7 in the UK, no.16 in Ireland and no.29 in Australia.

30 ~ Precious

UK: RCA 74321100257 (1992).
B-side: *Precious (Album Version)*.

6.06.92: 33-**23**-27-42-67

Australia
29.06.92: peaked at no.**77**, charted for 9 weeks

Belgium
4.07.92: 37-**27**-41-46

Germany
13.07.92: 68-60-**49**-62-58-72-74-81-81

Netherlands
6.06.92: 95-61-43-**39**-52-85

Sweden
24.06.92: 32-**28** (bi-weekly)

Switzerland
19.07.92: 40-x-**37**

Written by Annie, *Precious* was the second single released from her *DIVA* album, but it was as successful as *Why*.

Precious charted at no.23 in the UK, no.27 in Belgium, no.28 in Sweden, no.37 in Switzerland and no.39 in the Netherlands, and was a minor hit in Australia and Germany.

Annie also wrote *Step By Step*, one of the tracks featured on the maxi-CD release of *Precious*. *Step By Step* was later recorded by Whitney Houston ~ with Annie contributing backing vocals ~ for the original soundtrack album to the 1996 film, *The Preacher's Wife*, which co-starred Whitney alongside Denzel Washington.

Annie Lennox

A MOMENTUM THAT CAN'T BE BROKEN ...

Walking On Broken Glass

"WALKING ON BROKEN GLASS" IS THE NEXT DYNAMIC SINGLE AND FOLLOW-UP TO "WHY", HER FIRST MULTI-FORMAT SMASH.

FROM HER STUNNING SOLO PLATINUM DEBUT ALBUM

DIVA

BMG

31 ~ Walking On Broken Glass

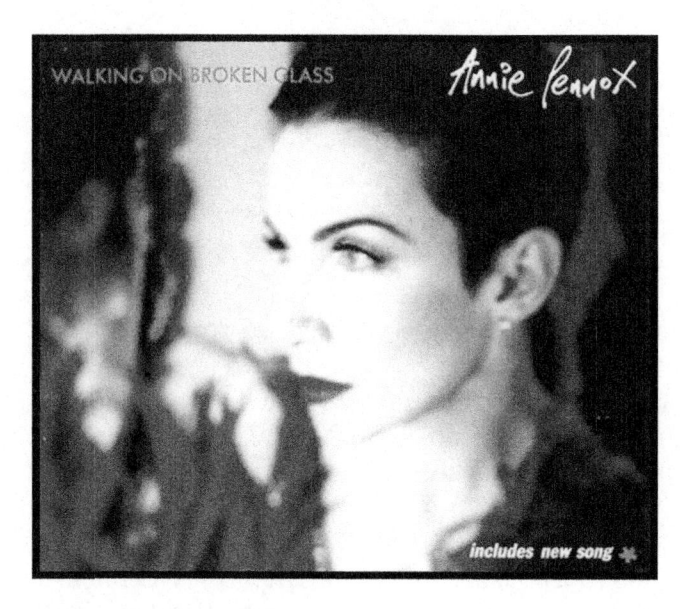

UK: RCA 74321107227 (1992).
B-side: *Legend In My Living Room.*

22.08.92: 23-9-**8**-9-12-18-29-60
21.03.09: 76-100

Australia
14.09.92: peaked at no.**62**, charted for 14 weeks

Belgium
26.09.92: **37**-**37**-43-45

Germany
28.09.92: 57-**51**-53-56-52-53-53-53-54-60-64-63-59-59-78-66-70-82

Ireland
24.08.92: 29-16-**8**-13-14-18

Netherlands
22.08.92: 100-78-69-**61**-72

New Zealand
25.10.92: 30-**23**-31-31-29-x-41

Sweden
30.09.92: **31** (bi-weekly)

USA
5.09.92: 96-71-65-49-38-30-28-22-21-17-**14**-16-16-18-17-19-20-22-27-26-24-35-39-43-49

Zimbabwe
24.10.92: peaked at no.**8**, charted for 3 weeks

Walking On Broken Glass, like *Why* and *Precious*, was composed by Annie ~ it was issued as the third single from her album, *DIVA*.

Walking On Broken Glass proved more popular than *Precious*, and rose to no.8 in Ireland, the UK and Zimbabwe, no.14 in the USA, no.23 in New Zealand, no.31 in Sweden and no.37 in Belgium, but it was only a minor hit in Australia, Germany and the Netherlands.

On the various CD single releases of *Walking On Broken Glass*, Annie included her versions of Ike & Tina Turner's 1966 hit, *River Deep, Mountain High*, plus Lennon & McCartney's *Don't Let Me Down*, which was released as the B-side to the Beatles' single *Get Back* in 1969.

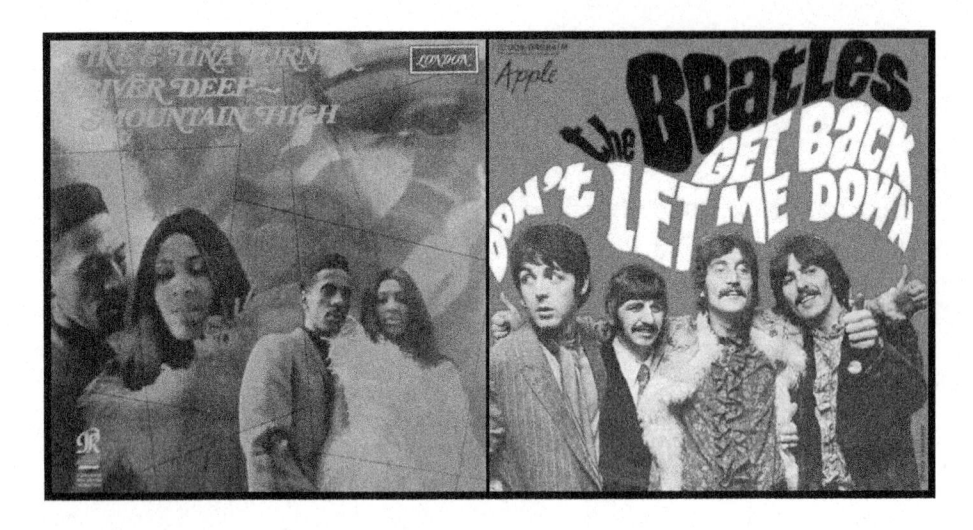

32 ~ Cold

UK: RCA 74321116902 (1992).
 Tracks: *Why/The Gift/Walking On Broken Glass*.

31.10.92: **26**-39-58-71

Australia
4.01.93: peaked at no.**80**, charted for 3 weeks

Belgium
21.11.92: **46**

Netherlands
31.10.92: 95-82-74-63-55-**51**-85

Cold was the fourth single released from Annie's *DIVA* album, and although it failed to match the sales of the previous three, it is notable as the first single not to be released on vinyl to enter the Top 40 in the UK.

Three different CD singles were released, themed Cold, Colder and Coldest, each with different bonus tracks, which were all recorded live during Annie's MTV Unplugged appearance in July 1992. The bonus tracks were:

- Cold: *Why/The Gift/Walking On Broken Glass*

- Colder: *It's Alright (Baby's Coming Back)/Here Comes The Rain Again/You Have Placed A Chill In My Heart*

ANNIE LENNOX

COLD＋アンプラグド・ライブ
アニー・レノックス
CD BOX 限定10,000セット

これが最初で最後?!!

アニーの初のライブ・テイクが収められたが日本特別CDボックスがこれ!! '92年7月に行なわれたMTV アンプラグドのアコースティックライブがこの3枚に収められている本盤イギリスではゴールドのシングル盤として別々に発売されている3枚を日本のみボックスとしてまとめたものだ。

COLD **COLDER** **COLDEST**

1/21 ON SALE

発売元：BMGビクター株式会社

- Coldest: *River Deep, Mountain High/Feel The Need/Don't Let Me Down*

Feel The Need was a hit for the Detroit Emeralds in 1977.

Cold made its chart debut in the UK at no.26, but it rose no higher. The single was also a minor hit in Australia, Belgium and the Netherlands, but it missed the chart in many countries.

Gary
OLDMAN
Winona
RYDER
Anthony
HOPKINS
Keanu
REEVES
BRAM STOKER
Dracula

33 ~ Little Bird / Love Song For A Vampire

UK: RCA 74321128837 (1993).
Double A-Side.

13.02.93: **3-3-3-3**-5-7-12-17-25-29-41-63
25.08.12: 96 (*Little Bird*)

Australia
21.03.93: 44-46-46-41-40-**38**-48-41

France
13.02.93: 34-32-25-17-16-15-**10-10**-15-18-41-22-40-49-36 (*Love Song For A Vampire*)

Germany
8.03.93: 100-41-31-30-**29**-30-32-37-42-46-77-83

Ireland
8.02.93: 25-7-**3-3-3**-4-5-5-11-15-24

New Zealand
11.04.93: **33** (*Little Bird*)

Spain
19.04.93: peaked at no.**4**, charted for 11 weeks (*Love Song For A Vampire*)

Switzerland
7.03.93: 35-40-**34**-**34**

USA
23.01.93: 86-78-71-67-59-54-51-**49**-52-66-79-99 (*Little Bird*)

Little Bird was the fifth and final single lifted from Annie's debut solo album, *DIVA*. In some countries, it was issued as a double A-side with *Love Song For A Vampire*. Annie composed both songs herself.

Annie was heavily pregnant with her second daughter Tali, when she filmed the music video for *Little Bird*, which Sophie Muller directed. In the promo, Annie played a ringmaster and appeared alongside eight lookalikes, each dressed as a different persona from one of her previous videos, both solo and with Eurythmics.

On its own, *Little Bird* charted at no.33 in New Zealand and no.49 in the USA.

Annie performed *Little Bird* at the closing ceremony of the 2012 Summer Olympic Games, staged in London, on 12th August 2012. As a result, *Little Bird* re-entered the UK chart for a solitary week at no.96.

Annie recorded *Love Song for A Vampire* for the 1992 film, *Bram Stoker's Dracula*, based on the popular 1897 novel. The song played over the film's end credits, and featured on the accompanying soundtrack album.

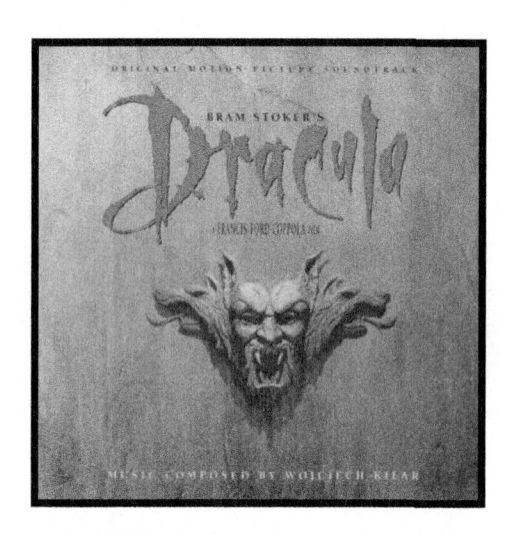

Love Song For A Vampire charted at no.4 in Spain and no.10 in France.

As a double A-side, *Little Bird/Love Song For A Vampire* spent four weeks at no.3 in the UK, and three weeks at no.3 in Ireland. The single wasn't quite as successful elsewhere, peaking at no.29 in Germany, no.34 in Switzerland and no.38 in Australia.

34 ~ No More "I Love You's"

UK: RCA 74321257162 (1995).
Tracks: *Ladies Of The Canyon/Love Song For A Vampire*.

18.02.95: **2-2**-4-6-12-23-36-54-60-61-69-75-x-x-99
21.03.09: 91

Australia
19.02.95: 35-27-17-18-**16**-17-17-17-25034038-42-45-50

Austria
19.03.95: **11-11**-17-14-12-15-17-15-25-27

Belgium
25.02.95: 50-39-28-**27**-43

Denmark
17.02.95: 15-**8**-14-20-15-15

France
18.03.95: 30-31-24-20-18-**13**-16-20-16-17-24-38-44-48

Germany
13.03.95: 61-51-33-28-**27**-31-37-43-60-52-55-58-61-63-73-82

Ireland
9.02.95: 10-**2**-3-3-8-9-18-27

Netherlands
18.02.95: 34-22-**17-17**-24-35

New Zealand
12.03.95: 23-**22**-23-33-24-37-36-43-45

Norway
25.02.95: 13-**12**-13-14-17-13-19-**12**-20

Spain
13.02.95: peaked at no.**1** (1), charted for 9 weeks

Sweden
17.02.95: 21-**15**-18-20-27-34

Switzerland
19.03.95: 21-**14**-21-27-26-31-26-26-29-29-29-x-35-x-47

USA
11.03.95: 78-61-56-52-46-34-32-31-31-29-27-**23-23-23**-25-30-37-37-42-47-45

Zimbabwe
17.04.95: peaked at no.**4**, charted for 14 weeks

No More "I Love You's" was written by David Freeman and Joseph Hughes, who recorded the song as the duo The Lover Speaks, for their self-titled debut album, released in 1986.

The Lover Speaks scored a minor no.58 in the UK with *No More "I Love You's"*.

With slightly altered lyrics, Annie recorded a cover of *No More "I Love You's"* for her second solo album, *MEDUSA*.

'There are quite a few songs floating around,' said Annie, speaking in 1995, 'which should have touched the consciousness of the nation ~ they should have made their mark, and this is one of them. I might be sticking my neck out to do this, but I really wanted to give it another chance because it's a magnificent song. The lyrics are extraordinary, poetic and abstract ~ the perfect sort of vehicle for me.'

'When Annie Lennox covered *No More "I Love You's"*,' said co-writer David Freeman, 'she nailed it! She has the ability to be camp and soulful. We were very lucky that she recorded our song.'

No More "I Love You's" was released as the lead single from *MEDUSA*, and gave Annie her biggest solo success to date. It hit no.1 in Spain, no.2 in Ireland and the UK, no.4 in Zimbabwe, no.8 in Denmark, no.11 in Austria, no.12 in Norway, no.13 in France, no.14 in Switzerland, no.15 in Sweden, no.16 in Australia, no.17 in the Netherlands, no.22 in New Zealand, no.23 in the USA, and no.27 in Belgium and Germany.

Annie won a Grammy Award for *No More "I Love You's"*, for Best Pop Vocal Performance, Female.

Annie's version of *No More "I Love You's"* was sampled by American rapper and singer Nicki Minaj on her 2010 single *Your Love*, which charted at no.14 in the USA and no.43 in Canada.

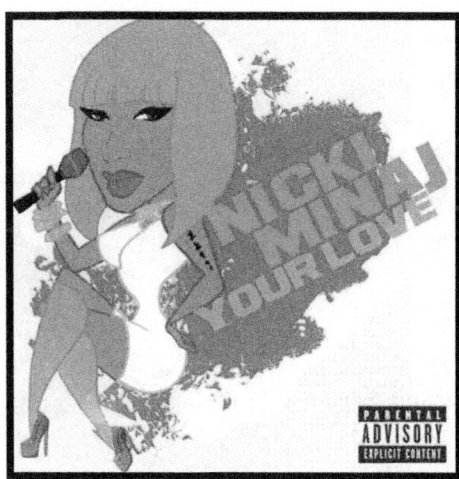

35 ~ A Whiter Shade Of Pale

UK: RCA 74321284822 (1995).
Tracks: *Heaven/(I'm Always Touched By Your) Presence Dear/Love Song For A Vampire.*

10.06.95: **16**-18-21-39-56-68-76-95

Australia
22.06.95: peaked at no.**56**, charted for 6 weeks

Belgium
24.06.95: **48**-50

France
2.09.95: 49-45-36-40-36-39-33-**17**-23-20-21-21-28-34-40-x-50

Germany
17.07.95: **77**-98-84-82-88-85-86-89-99-100

Ireland
15.06.95: **25**-25

Netherlands
15.07.95: 47-**39**-39

Switzerland
25.06.95: 39-34-**26**-35-46-27-33-41-44-49

A Whiter Shade Of Pale was written by Gary Brooker, Keith Reid and Matthew Fisher, and was originally recorded by Procol Harem for their self-titled debut album, released in 1967.

Released as the band's debut single, *A Whiter Shade Of Pale* was a huge success globally: it hit no.1 in numerous countries, including Australia, Belgium, Canada, France, Germany, Ireland, Italy, New Zealand, Spain and the UK. The single also achieved no.3 in Norway, no.4 in Austria and no.5 in the USA.

Annie's cover of *A Whiter Shade Of Pale*, which she recorded for her *MEDUSA* album, was released as the follow-up to *No More "I Love You's"*, but it proved less successful. Nevertheless, it charted at no.16 in the UK, no.17 in France, no.25 in Ireland, no.26 in Switzerland, no.37 in Canada, no.39 in the Netherlands, and was a minor hit in Australia, Belgium and Germany.

36 ~ Waiting In Vain

UK: RCA 74321316122 (1995).
  Tracks: *Train In Vain (T's Mix)/(Dan's Monster Club Mix)/(Guru Mix)*.

30.09.95: **31**-47-66-91

Waiting In Vain was composed by Bob Marley, and was originally recorded by Bob Marley & The Wailers for their 1977 album, *EXODUS*.

Released as a single, Bob Marley & The Wailers took *Waiting In Vain* to no.27 in the UK and no.38 in New Zealand.

Annie recorded a cover of *Waiting In Vain* for *MEDUSA*, and it was issued as the album's third single. However, the only country where it achieved Top 40 status was the UK, where it made its chart debut at its peak position, no.31 ~ four places shy of what the Bob Marley & The Wailers original had achieved.

Annie's version of *Waiting In Vain* featured in the 2001 film, *Serendipity*, and in the 2002 film, *Changing Lanes*.

Step By Step by Whitney Houston

UK: Arista 74321 44933 2 (1996).
Tracks: *Step By Step (Album Version)/(Teddy Riley Remix)/(K-Klassic Mix)*.

21.12.96: 17-15-15-**13**-18-17-16-22-26-25-37-41-63-87

Australia
19.01.97: 17-17-13-13-14-**12**-14-18-14-14-17-18-17-29-40

Austria
12.01.97: 33-32-15-10-8-**6**-8-**6-6**-10-8-9-18-13-19-27

Belgium
11.01.97: 40-30-27-19-19-15-15-16-**12**-19-24-29-35-36

Denmark
20.12.96: 14-7-**6-6-6-6**-7-11-12-13-15-14-14-20

Finland
18.01.97: 12-**11**

France
18.01.97: 36-42-34-34-33-**30**-32-47-38

Germany
16.12.96: 67-41-41-34-28-20-10-**8-8**-10-9-11-13-15-17-18-29-32-42-50-54-55

Ireland
2.01.97: 26-19-**14**-17-19-19-23-23-29

Netherlands
21.12.96: 75-53-52-40-27-20-17-**13**-16-18-18-18-19-23-24-31-38-49-64-74-78-81-95

New Zealand
16.02.97: 49-x-**46**-49

Sweden
20.12.96: 45-36-34-20-18-**15**-34-27-47-46-52

Switzerland
2.02.97: 20-20-19-**15-15**-21-19-19-20-26-31-33-42-49-43

USA
15.03.97: 22-**15**-17-17-22-31-37-43-56-60-65-80-79-86-88-97-100

Annie wrote and originally recorded *Step By Step* ~ it featured on some formats of her 1992 single, *Precious*.

With some new lyrics, and with Annie contributing backing vocals, Whitney Houston recorded *Step By Step* for the 1996 film, *The Preacher's Wife*, which saw Whitney playing the title role. Two versions, including a remix by Teddy Riley, featured on the accompanying soundtrack album.

Outside North America and Australasia, Whitney's cover of *Step By Step* was chosen as the lead single from *THE PREACHER'S WIFE*. It achieved no.3 in Spain, no.6 in Austria and Denmark, no.8 in Germany, no.11 in Finland, no.13 in Belgium, the Netherlands and the UK, no.14 in Ireland and Italy, no.15 in Sweden and Switzerland, no.30 in France and no.46 in New Zealand.

In North America and Australasia, the lead single from *THE PREACHER'S WIFE* was *I Believe In You And Me*, with *Step By Step* issued as the follow-up. *Step By Step* rose to no.15 on the Hot 100 in the USA, and peaked at no.11 in Australia and no.23 in Canada.

27 ~ I Saved The World Today by Eurythmics

UK: BMG/RCA/19 Management Ltd 74321695632 (1999).
B-side: *I Saved The World Today (Live At The Church)/Lifted*

16.10.99: **11**-18-28-41-53-68-84-100

Australia
5.12.99: **85**

Austria
17.10.99: 36-25-**18**-20-19-22-24-35

Belgium
16.10.99: 49-**36**-40-43-49

Finland
2.10.99: 3-3-**2**-5-7

Germany
18.10.99: 46-51-44-40-31-34-38-**28**-35-37-46-46-54-63

Ireland
7.10.99: 35-27-**23**-26-33-38

Netherlands
9.10.99: 85-50-**44**-44-52-54-63-71-68-69-69-84

New Zealand
5.12.99: 48-47-48-x-x-x-40-41-**33**-36-45-42

Spain
11.10.99: 18-**16-16**-17-19

Sweden
7.10.99: 54-**31**-34-35-36-50-41-45

Switzerland
24.10.99: 18-**16**-17-20-26-27-27-28-28-34-36-41-42-52-60-83-64

Written by Annie and Dave Stewart, *I Saved The World Today* was the first new Eurythmics single to be released for almost a decade, following Annie and Dave going their separate ways after their *WE TOO ARE ONE* album appeared. The duo recorded the track for a brand new Eurythmics album, *PEACE*.

'It's a beautiful song,' said Annie, 'but it contains something dark at the centre.'

Surprisingly, *I Saved The World Today* wasn't released as a single in North America, but it was a hit in many other countries, charting at no.2 in France, no.11 in the UK, no.16 in Spain and Switzerland, no.18 in Austria, no.23 in Ireland, no.28 in Germany, no.31 in Sweden, no.33 in New Zealand, no.36 in Belgium and no.44 in the Netherlands.

38 ~ 17 Again by Eurythmics

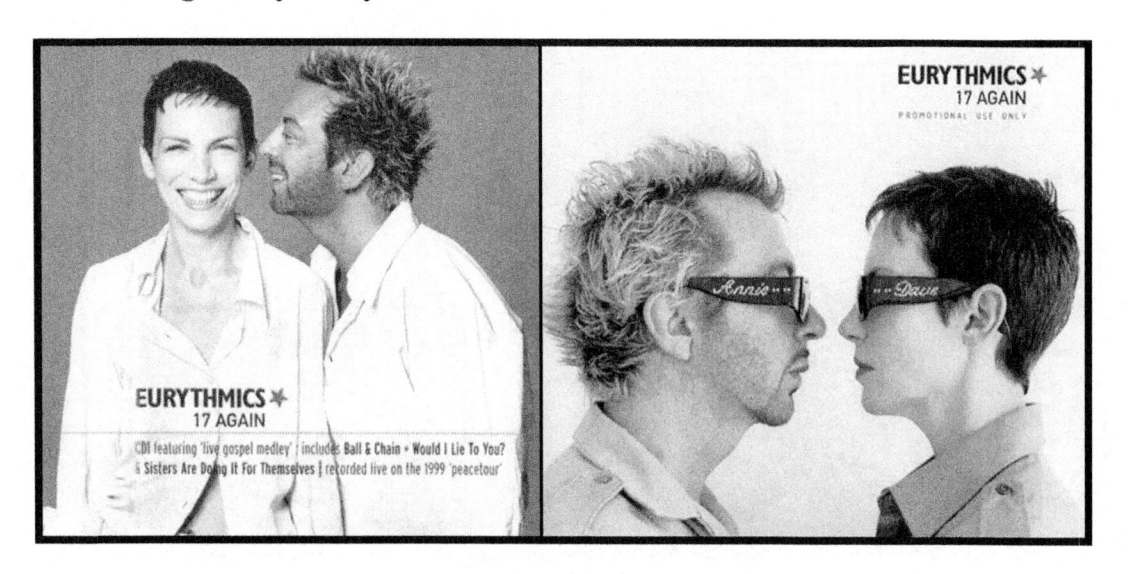

UK: BMG/RCA/19 Management Ltd 74321726262 (1999).
  B-side: *Gospel Medley (Ball & Chain/Would I Lie To You?/Sisters Are Doin' It For Themselves)*.

5.02.00: **27**-44-52-67-100-x-x-99-84

Germany
7.02.00: **73**-86-87-90-95-100

Ireland
27.01.00: **43**-45

Switzerland
13.02.00: 70-x-**67**-81-96-96

17 Again, composed by Annie and Dave Stewart, was the second single released from the Eurythmics album *PEACE* in most countries, but it failed to match the success of *I Saved The World Today*. It achieved no.27 in the UK and no.43 in Ireland, and was a minor hit in Germany and Switzerland, but it failed to chart in many countries.

Although not given full single release, promotional remixes of *17 Again* were issued to nightclubs in the United States, and the track gave Eurythmics their first no.1 on Billboard's Hot Dance Club Play chart. However, not having approved it, Annie and Dave had the remix that topped the dance chart withdrawn.

39 ~ I've Got A Life by Eurythmics

UK: RCA/Sony BMG Music 82876748342 (2005).
B-side: *Sweet Dreams (Are Made Of This) (Steve Angello Mix)*.

12.11.05: **14**-32-44-69

Ireland
12.11.05: **38**-49

Switzerland
20.11.05: **36**-43-75-84-95-97

Written by Annie and Dave Stewart, *I've Got A Life* was one of two new songs the duo recorded during the *PEACE* album sessions, but failed to make the album. It was one of two previously unreleased tracks from the sessions included on the 2005 Eurythmics compilation, ULTIMATE COLLECTION (the other, *Was It Just Another Love Affair?*, wasn't issued as a single).

The music video for *I've Got A Life*, directed by Matthew Rolston, saw Annie and Dave performing the song in front of TV screens showing promos spanning the duo's entire career with Eurythmics.

I've Got A Life is the most recent Eurythmics single, but it wasn't a major success, peaking at no.14 in the UK, no.36 in Switzerland and no.38 in Ireland, but failing to chart in most countries.

40 ~ Shining Light

UK: RCA Digital Release (2009).

14.03.09: 50-**39**-58-92

Written by Tim Wheeler, *Shining Light* was originally recorded by the Irish rock band, Ash, for their 2000 album, *FREE ALL ANGELS*.

Released as the album's lead single, Ash took *Shining Light* to no.8 in the UK and no.23 in Ireland.

'It's a very melodic song,' said Ash's Rick McMurray, 'it sticks in your head, so we thought it'd have a pretty good chance of getting in the Top 10. It was good being back there 'cos it's been a long time, over two years since we had a single out.'

Shining Light was one of two new songs Annie recorded for her 2009 compilation, THE ANNIE LENNOX COLLECTION. It wasn't released as a physical single, but was made available to download, which helped it to no.39 in the UK ~ however, it missed the chart in most countries.

Annie promoted *Shining Light* with a video where she fronts an all-female band, in which she played all the band members.

The song's composer, Tim Wheeler, approved of Annie's version of *Shining Light*.

'It's cool, I'm really into it,' he said. 'It makes me proud that someone of her stature and talent is doing something different with our song.'

VVV MAGAZINE

THE
CONVICTION
ISSUE

CINDY CRAWFORD | NOOMI RAPACE
CARMEN ELECTRA | TASHA TILBERG

Annie Lennox
ANNIE LENNOX

41 ~ I Put A Spell On You

UK: Island Records Digital Release (2015).

I Put A Spell On You wasn't a hit in the UK.

Australia
1.03.15: **81**

Austria
27.02.15: 65-**60**-74

France
21.02.15: 35-**29**-44-59-74-76

Germany
27.02.15: 81-**63**-77

Sweden
27.02.15: **81**

Switzerland
22.02.15: 51-**44**-46

I Put A Spell On You was composed and originally recorded by Jalacy 'Screamin' Jay' Hawkins in 1956.

Annie recorded a cover of *I Put A Spell On You* for her 2014 album, *NOSTALGIA*. Promoted as a single, she took the song to no.29 in France and no.44 in Switzerland, but it was only a minor hit in Australia, Austria, Germany and Sweden, and failed to chart in many countries, including the UK.

Numerous versions of *I Put A Spell On You* have been recorded over the years, and several artists have charted with their version, including:

- Alan Price Set ~ no.9 in the UK in 1966.
- Creedence Clearwater Revival ~ no.58 in the USA in 1968.
- Bryan Ferry ~ no.18 in the UK in 1993.
- Sonique ~ no.36 in the UK in 1998, and no.8 when reissued two years later.

THE ALMOST TOP 40 SINGLES

Three singles, all credited to Annie Lennox, have made the Top 50 in one or more countries, but failed to enter the Top 40 in any.

Something So Right

Something So Right was written and originally recorded by Paul Simon, for his 1973 album, *THERE GOES RHYMIN' SIMON*. Annie recorded a cover of the song for her 1995 album, *MEDUSA*, and later the same year she re-recorded the song with Paul Simon. This version, with the credit 'Guest Vocals Paul Simon', was issued as a single in Europe. It made its chart debut in the UK at no.44, but climbed no higher, and wasn't a hit anywhere else.

Dark Road

Annie wrote and recorded *Dark Road* for her 2007 solo album, *SONGS OF MASS DESTRUCTION*. Released as the album's lead single, *Dark Road* sold poorly ~ it achieved no.45 in Switzerland and no.58 in the UK, but failed to chart in most countries.

Many Rivers To Cross

Jimmy Cliff wrote and originally recorded *Many Rivers To Cross*, for his self-titled 1969 album. Over the years, numerous artists have covered the song, including Bryan Adams, Harry Nilsson, Joe Cocker, John Lennon, Linda Ronstadt, Percy Sledge and UB40.

Annie performed *Many Rivers To Cross* at the American charitable concert, *Idol Gives Back*, in 2008, and this live recording featured on the bonus disc that came with the limited edition version of her 2009 compilation, *THE ANNIE LENNOX COLLECTION*.

Made available digitally, Annie's version of *Many Rivers To Cross* charted at no.47 in Ireland, and was a minor no.80 hit in the USA, but it wasn't a hit anywhere else.

Note: to date, no albums by The Tourists, Eurythmics or Annie Lennox have achieved Top 50 status in one or more countries, but failed to enter the Top 40 in any.

ANNIE'S TOP 30 SINGLES

In this Top 30, each of Annie's singles has been scored according to the following points system.

Points are given according to the peak position reached on the singles chart in each of the countries featured in this book:

- No.1: 100 points for the first week at no.1, plus 10 points for each additional week at no.1.

- No.2: 90 points for the first week at no.2, plus 5 points for each additional week at no.2.

- No.3: 85 points.
- No.4-6: 80 points.
- No.7-10: 75 points.
- No.11-15: 70 points.
- No.16-20: 65 points.
- No.21-30: 60 points.
- No.31-40: 50 points.
- No.41-50: 40 points.
- No.51-60: 30 points.
- No.61-70: 20 points.
- No.71-80: 10 points.
- No.81-100: 5 points.

Total weeks charted in each country are added, to give the final points score.

Reissues, re-entries and remixes of a single are counted together.

Rank/Single/Points

1 *There Must Be An Angel (Playing With My Heart)* – 1654 points

2 *Sweet Dreams (Are Made Of This)* – 1562 points

3 *No More "I Love You's"* – 1334 points

4 *Why* – 1174 points

Rank/Single/Points

5. *Sexcrime (Nineteen Eighty-Four) – 1082 points*

6. *When Tomorrow Comes* – 1022 points
7. *Here Comes The Rain Again* – 999 points
8. *Thorn In My Side* – 983 points
9. *Would I Lie To You?* – 980 points
10. *Beethoven (I Love To Listen To)* – 968 points

11. *Put A Little Love In Your Heart* – 913 points
12. *Sisters Are Doin' It For Themselves* – 900 points
13. *Love Is A Stranger* – 868 points
14. *Revival* – 860 points
15. *Who's That Girl?* – 795 points

16. *I Saved The World Today* – 768 points
17. *The Miracle Of Love* – 760 points
18. *Right By Your Side* – 716 points
19. *It's Alright (Baby's Coming Back)* – 707 points
20. *Little Bird/Love Song For A Vampire* – 662 points

21. *Walking On Broken Glass* – 618 points
22. *Missionary Man* – 541 points
23. *Don't Ask Me Why* – 536 points
24. *A Whiter Shade Of Pale* – 442 points
25. *Shame* – 442 points

26. *I Need A Man* – 398 points
27. *Precious* – 369 points
28. *The King And Queen Of America* – 294 points
29. *I Only Want To Be With You* – 270 points
30. *You Have Placed A Chill In My Heart* – 233 points

Annie's Top 30 features 22 singles by Eurythmics, seven by Annie solo and one by The Tourists.

There Must Be An Angel (Playing With My Heart) narrowly emerges as Annie's most successful single, ahead of *Sweet Dreams (Are Made Of This)*. Two solo efforts by Annie come next, with *No More "I Love You's"* taking third place, just ahead of *Why*. Another Eurythmics hit, *Sexcrime (Nineteen Eighty-Four)*, rounds off the Top 5.

The Tourists make the Top 30, just, with their cover of *I Only Want To Be With You*, which sneaks in at no.29.

SINGLES TRIVIA

To date, Annie Lennox has achieved forty-one Top 40 singles in one or more of the countries featured in this book, 26 with Eurythmics, 11 solo and four as part of The Tourists. There follows a country-by-country look at her most successful hits.

Note: in the past, there was often one or more weeks over Christmas and New Year when no new chart was published in some countries. In such cases, the previous week's chart has been used to complete chart runs. Similarly, where a bi-weekly or monthly chart was in place, for chart runs these are counted as two and four weeks, respectively.

ANNIE IN AUSTRALIA

Most Hits

21 hits	Eurythmics
9 hits	Annie Lennox
1 hit	The Tourists

Most Weeks

291 weeks	Eurythmics
84 weeks	Annie Lennox
19 weeks	The Tourists

No.1 Singles

1985   *Would I Lie To You?*

Would I Lie To You? topped the chart for two weeks.

Singles with the most weeks

22 weeks	*Love Is A Stranger*
22 weeks	*Thorn In My Side*
21 weeks	*Would I Lie To You?*
19 weeks	*I Only Want To Be With You*
19 weeks	*Sweet Dreams (Are Made Of This)*
18 weeks	*Who's That Girl?*
18 weeks	*Right By Your Side*
18 weeks	*Sexcrime (Nineteen Eighty-Four)*

18 weeks	*When Tomorrow Comes*
17 weeks	*There Must Be An Angel (Playing With My Heart)*
17 weeks	*Put A Little Love In Your Heart*

ANNIE IN AUSTRIA

Most Hits

5 hits	Eurythmics
4 hits	Annie Lennox

Most Weeks

44 weeks	Eurythmics
41 weeks	Annie Lennox

Annie's most successful single in Austria is *Put A Little Love In Your Heart*, her duet with Al Green, which peaked at no.4.

Most weeks

16 weeks	*Put A Little Love In Your Heart*
12 weeks	*Thorn In My Side*
12 weeks	*Why*
10 weeks	*There Must Be An Angel (Playing With My Heart)*
10 weeks	*No More "I Love You's"*

ANNIE IN BELGIUM (Flanders)

Most Hits

21 hits	Eurythmics
7 hits	Annie Lennox

Most Weeks

115 weeks	Eurythmics
37 weeks	Annie Lennox

Annie's most successful singles in Belgium are *Sweet Dreams (Are Made Of This)* and *Sexcrime (Nineteen Eighty-Four)*, which both peaked at no.3.

Most weeks

11 weeks	*Love Is A Stranger*
11 weeks	*Sexcrime (Nineteen Eighty-Four)*
11 weeks	*Why*
10 weeks	*Sweet Dreams (Are Made Of This)*
10 weeks	*There Must Be An Angel (Playing With My Heart)*
10 weeks	*When Tomorrow Comes*
10 weeks	*Put A Little Love In Your Heart*
9 weeks	*Revival*
8 weeks	*Would I Lie To You?*

ANNIE IN CANADA

Most Hits

13 hits	Eurythmics
1 hit	Annie Lennox

Most Weeks

162 weeks	Eurythmics
14 weeks	Annie Lennox

No.1 Singles

1983   *Sweet Dreams (Are Made Of This)*

Sweet Dreams (Are Made Of This) topped the chart for three weeks.

Singles with the most weeks

22 weeks	*Sweet Dreams (Are Made Of This)*
19 weeks	*There Must Be An Angel (Playing With My Heart)*
17 weeks	*Would I Lie To You?*
15 weeks	*I Need A Man*
15 weeks	*Don't Ask Me Why*
14 weeks	*Missionary Man*
14 weeks	*Put A Little Love In My Heart*
13 weeks	*Here Comes The Rain Again*
12 weeks	*Sexcrime (Nineteen Eighty-Four)*
10 weeks	*Love Is A Stranger*

Note: this information relates to pre-1997 only.

ANNIE IN DENMARK

Most Hits

4 hits	Eurythmics
2 hit	Annie Lennox

Most Weeks

24 weeks	Eurythmics
8 weeks	Annie Lennox

Annie's most successful single in Denmark is *Beethoven (I Love To Listen To)*, which peaked at no.4.

Singles with the most weeks

7 weeks	*When Tomorrow Comes*
6 weeks	*Thorn In My Side*
6 weeks	*Revival*
6 weeks	*No More "I Love You's"*
5 weeks	*Beethoven (I Love To Listen To)*

ANNIE IN FINLAND

Most Hits

8 hits	Eurythmics

Most Weeks

45 weeks	Eurythmics

Annie's most successful singles in Finland are *There Must Be An Angel (Playing With My Heart)* and *I Saved The World Today*, which both peaked at no.2.

Singles with the most weeks

8 weeks	*There Must Be An Angel (Playing With My Heart)*
8 weeks	*When Tomorrow Comes*

8 weeks   *Thorn In My Side*
5 weeks   *I Saved The World Today*

ANNIE IN FRANCE

Most Hits

6 hits   Eurythmics
4 hits   Annie Lennox

Most Weeks

64 weeks   Eurythmics
51 weeks   Annie Lennox

Annie's most successful single in France is *Sexcrime (Nineteen Eighty-Four)*, which peaked at no.7.

Singles with the most weeks

19 weeks   *Sexcrime (Nineteen Eighty-Four)*
16 weeks   *A Whiter Shade Of Pale*
15 weeks   *There Must Be An Angel (Playing With My Heart)*
15 weeks   *Love Song For A Vampire*
14 weeks   *The Miracle Of Love*
14 weeks   *No More "I Love You's"*
11 weeks   *Sweet Dreams (Are Made Of This) (Remix)*

ANNIE IN GERMANY

Most Hits

20 hits   Eurythmics
 8 hits   Annie Lennox

Most weeks

244 weeks   Eurythmics
 98 weeks   Annie Lennox

Annie's most successful single in Germany is *Sexcrime (Nineteen Eighty-Four)*, which peaked at no.3.

Most weeks

26 weeks	*Love Is A Stranger*
23 weeks	*Sweet Dreams (Are Made Of This)*
19 weeks	*Why*
18 weeks	*Walking On Broken Glass*
16 weeks	*Sexcrime (Nineteen Eighty-Four)*
16 weeks	*No More "I Love You's"*
14 weeks	*Here Comes The Rain Again*
14 weeks	*There Must Be An Angel (Playing With My Heart)*
14 weeks	*Thorn In My Side*
14 weeks	*Revival*
14 weeks	*I Saved The World Today*

ANNIE IN IRELAND

Most Hits

25 hits	Eurythmics
7 hits	Annie Lennox
2 hits	The Tourists

Most Weeks

91 weeks	Eurythmics
34 weeks	Annie Lennox
9 weeks	The Tourists

No.1 Singles

1985   *There Must Be An Angel (Playing With My Heart)*

There Must Be An Angel (Playing With My Heart) topped the chart for one week.

Singles with the most weeks

11 weeks	*Little Bird/Love Song for A Vampire*
8 weeks	*No More "I Love You's"*
7 weeks	*So Good To Be Back Home Again*
7 weeks	*Sexcrime (Nineteen Eighty-Four)*
7 weeks	*There Must Be An Angel (Playing With My Heart)*
7 weeks	*Thorn In My Side*
6 weeks	*Who's That Girl?*

6 weeks   *Walking On Broken Glass*
6 weeks   *I Saved The World Today*

ANNIE IN JAPAN

Annie, with Eurythmics, only achieved one minor hit single in Japan: *Sweet Dreams (Are Made Of This)* achieved no.89, and charted for 4 weeks.

ANNIE IN THE NETHERLANDS

Most Hits

19 hits   Eurythmics
 7 hits   Annie Lennox

Most Weeks

145 weeks   Eurythmics
 53 weeks   Annie Lennox

Annie's most successful single in the Netherlands is *There Must Be An Angel (Playing With My Heart)*, which peaked at no.3.

Singles with the most weeks

15 weeks   *Why*
13 weeks   *Sexcrime (Nineteen Eighty-Four)*
12 weeks   *There Must Be An Angel (Playing With My Heart)*
12 weeks   *I Saved The World Today*
11 weeks   *Put A Little Love In Your Heart*
10 weeks   *Revival*
 9 weeks   *Sweet Dreams (Are Made Of This)*
 9 weeks   *Beethoven (I Love To Listen To)*
 9 weeks   *The Kind And Queen Of America*

ANNIE IN NEW ZEALAND

Most Hits

20 hits   Eurythmics
 5 hits   Annie Lennox

Most Weeks

226 weeks   Eurythmics
 41 weeks   Annie Lennox

Annie's most successful single in New Zealand is *Sweet Dreams (Are Made Of This)*, which peaked at no.2.

Most weeks

20 weeks   *Who's That Girl?*
19 weeks   *Missionary Man*
17 weeks   *Love Is A Stranger*
17 weeks   *Sweet Dreams (Are Made Of This)*
17 weeks   *Sexcrime (Nineteen Eighty-Four)*
16 weeks   *Put A Little Love In Your Heart*
15 weeks   *Would I Lie To You?*
14 weeks   *Beethoven (I Love To Listen To)*
12 weeks   *There Must Be An Angel (Playing With My Heart)*
12 weeks   *Sisters Are Doin' It For Themselves*

ANNIE IN NORWAY

Most Hits

5 hits   Eurythmics
2 hits   Annie Lennox

Most Weeks

24 weeks   Eurythmics
11 weeks   Annie Lennox

No.1 Singles

1985   *There Must Be An Angel (Playing With My Heart)*

There Must Be An Angel (Playing With My Heart) topped the chart for one week.

Singles with the most weeks

9 weeks   *There Must Be An Angel (Playing With My Heart)*
9 weeks   *When Tomorrow Comes*

9 weeks   No More "I Love You's"
4 weeks   Beethoven (I Love To Listen To)
2 weeks   Why

ANNIE IN SOUTH AFRICA

Most Hits

5 hits   Eurythmics

Most Weeks

53 weeks   Eurythmics

Annie's most successful single in South Africa is *Love Is A Stranger*, which peaked at no.2.

Singles with the most weeks

19 weeks   *Love Is A Stranger*
14 weeks   *Sweet Dreams (Are Made Of This)*
13 weeks   *There Must Be An Angel (Playing With My Heart)*

ANNIE IN SPAIN

Most Hits

8 hits   Eurythmics
3 hits   Annie Lennox

Most Weeks

94 weeks   Eurythmics
25 weeks   Annie Lennox

No.1 Singles

1995   *No More "I Love You's"*

No More "I Love You's" topped the chart for one week.

Singles with the most weeks

25 weeks	*There Must Be An Angel (Playing With My Heart)*
16 weeks	*Sweet Dreams (Are Made Of This)*
16 weeks	*When Tomorrow Comes*
11 weeks	*The Miracle Of Love*
11 weeks	*Love Song For A Vampire*

ANNIE IN SWEDEN

Most Hits

12 hits	Eurythmics
5 hits	Annie Lennox

Most Weeks

92 weeks	Eurythmics
25 weeks	Annie Lennox

Annie's most successful single in Sweden is *There Must Be An Angel (Playing With My Heart)*, which peaked at no.2.

Singles with the most weeks

14 weeks	*There Must Be An Angel (Playing With My Heart)*
12 weeks	*Sexcrime (Nineteen Eighty-Four)*
12 weeks	*When Tomorrow Comes*
12 weeks	*Why*
8 weeks	*Who's That Girl*
8 weeks	*Would I Lie To You?*
8 weeks	*Thorn In My Side*
8 weeks	*Revival*
8 weeks	*I Saved The World Today*

ANNIE IN SWITZERLAND

Most Hits

13 hits	Eurythmics
8 hits	Annie Lennox

Most Weeks

92 weeks   Eurythmics
64 weeks   Annie Lennox

Annie's most successful singles in Switzerland are *Sexcrime (Nineteen Eighty-Four)* and *Why*, which both peaked at no.6.

Singles with the most weeks

21 weeks   *Why*
17 weeks   *I Saved The World Today*
13 weeks   *No More "I Love You's"*
12 weeks   *Sexcrime (Nineteen Eighty-Four)*
10 weeks   *Revival*
10 weeks   *A Whiter Shade Of Pale*
 9 weeks   *The Miracle Of Love*
 9 weeks   *Put A Little Love In Your Heart*

ANNIE IN THE UNITED KINGDOM

Most Hits

27 hits   Eurythmics
14 hits   Annie Lennox
 5 hits   The Tourists

Most weeks

236 weeks   Eurythmics
 91 weeks   Annie Lennox
 40 weeks   The Tourists

No.1 Singles

1985   *There Must Be An Angel (Playing With My Heart)*

There Must Be An Angel (Playing With My Heart) topped the chart for one week.

Singles with the most weeks

18 weeks   *Love Is A Stranger*
16 weeks   *Sweet Dreams (Are Made Of This)*

15 weeks	*Sexcrime (Nineteen Eighty-Four)*
14 weeks	*I Only Want To Be With You*
14 weeks	*No More 'I Love You's'*
13 weeks	*There Must Br An Angel (Playing With Your Heart)*
13 weeks	*Little Bird/Love Song For A Vampire*
12 weeks	*Sisters Are Doin' It For Themselves*
12 weeks	*Thorn In My Side*
11 weeks	*Right By Your Side*
11 weeks	*When Tomorrow Comes*
11 weeks	*The Miracle Of Love*
11 weeks	*Put A Little Love In Your Heart*

The BRIT Certified/BPI (British Phonographic Industry) Awards

The BPI began certifying Silver, Gold & Platinum singles in 1973. From 1973 to 1988: Silver = 250,000, Gold = 500,000 & Platinum = 1 million. From 1989 onwards: Silver = 200,000, Gold = 400,000 & Platinum = 600,000. Awards are based on shipments, not sales; however, in July 2013 the BPI automated awards, based on actual sales since February 1994.

Platinum	*Sweet Dreams (Are Made Of This)* (July 2018)	= 600,000
Gold	*I Only Want To Be With You* (January 1980)	= 500,000
Silver	*Here Comes The Rain Again* (January 1984)	= 250,000
Silver	*Sexcrime (Nineteen Eighty-Four)* (December 1984)	= 250,000
Silver	*Little Bird/Love Song For A Vampire* (March 1993)	= 200,000
Silver	*No More "I Love You's"* (February 1995)	= 200,000
Silver	*Walking On Broken Glass* (April 2019)	= 200,000

ANNIE IN THE UNITED STATES OF AMERICA

Most Hits

15 hits	Eurythmics
6 hits	Annie Lennox
1 hit	The Tourists

Most weeks

190 weeks	Eurythmics
96 weeks	Annie Lennox
4 weeks	The Tourists

No.1 Singles

1983   *Sweet Dreams (Are Made Of This)*

Sweet Dreams (Are Made Of This) spent one week at no.1.

Singles with the most weeks

26 weeks	*Sweet Dreams (Are Made Of This)*
25 weeks	*Walking On Broken Glass*
21 weeks	*No More 'I Love You's'*
20 weeks	*Here Comes The Rain Again*
20 weeks	*Why*
19 weeks	*Would I Lie To You?*
17 weeks	*Put A Little Love In Your Heart*
16 weeks	*Missionary Man*
15 weeks	*Sisters Are Doin' It For Themselves*
13 weeks	*Love Is A Stranger*
13 weeks	*Who's That Girl?*

RIAA (Recording Industry Association of America) Awards

The RIAA began certifying Gold singles in 1958 and Platinum singles in 1976. From 1958 to 1988: Gold = 1 million, Platinum = 2 million. From 1988 onwards: Gold = 500,000, Platinum = 1 million. Awards are based on shipments, not sales.

Gold   *Sweet Dreams (Are Made Of This)* (October 1983) = 1 million

ANNIE IN ZIMBABWE

Most Hits

5 hits	Eurythmics
2 hits	Annie Lennox

Most Weeks

47 weeks	Eurythmics
17 weeks	Annie Lennox

Annie's most successful single in Zimbabwe is *Right By Your Side*, which peaked at no.3.

Singles with the most weeks

14 weeks   *Right By Your Side*
14 weeks   *No More "I Love You's"*
13 weeks   *Sweet Dreams (Are Made Of This)*
10 weeks   *There Must Be An Angel (Playing With My Heart)*
 6 weeks   *Sisters Are Doin' It For Themselves*

All The Top 40 Albums

1 ~ REALITY EFFECT by The Tourists

It Doesn't Have To Be This Way/I Only Want To Be With You/In The Morning (When The Madness Has Faded)/All Life's Tragedies/Everywhere You Look/So Good To Be Back Home Again/Nothing To Do/Circular Fever/In My Mind (There's Sorrow)/Something In The Air Tonight/Summers Night

Produced by Tom Allom.

UK: Logo LOGO 1019 (1979).

3.11.79: 60-48-55-41-50-64-59-32-**23**-39-46-45-45-39-45-55

Australia
23.06.80: peaked at no.**62**, charted for 5 weeks

Canada
12.07.80: 97-93-89-**87**-95

Sweden
22.02.80: **45** (bi-weekly)

Zimbabwe
26.07.80: peaked at no.**18**

The self-titled debut album by The Tourists was released in June 1979; it spent a solitary week at no.72 in the UK, but failed to chart anywhere else.

The band's second album, *REALITY EFFECT*, was recorded at London's DMJ Studios and Olympic Studios, during August 1979 and was released two months later. Thanks to the success of the singles *I Only Want To Be With You* and *So Good To Be Back Home Again*, it gave the Tourists their first ~ and what proved to be their only ~ Top 40 album.

REALITY EFFECT charted at no.18 in Zimbabwe, no.23 in the UK and no.45 in Sweden, and was a minor hit in Australia.

The success of the album, and the singles lifted from it, brought The Tourists to the attention of Epic Records in North America. Here, the band's debut album, also rather confusingly titled *REALITY EFFECT*, was actually made up of tracks from both *THE TOURISTS* and *REALITY EFFECT*. The track listing was as follows:

It Doesn't Have To Be This Way/I Only Want To Be With You/Blind Among The Flowers/In The Morning (When The Madness Has Faded)/All Life's Tragedies/ Everywhere You Look/Nothing To Do/The Loneliest Man In The World/So Good To Be Back Home Again/Circular Fever/In My Mind (There's Sorrow)/Fool's Paradise

REALITY EFFECT was a minor no.87 hit in Canada, and rose to no.115 on the Billboard 200 in the United States.

'Personally, I was never 100% happy with our first two albums,' said Annie, 'but on our latest, *LUMINOUS BASEMENT*, it's definitely all there. Hopefully, we will continue improving on every album we make. As long as you want to keep working, and you're enjoying it, you forge ahead.'

LUMINOUR BASEMENT, which charted for one week at no.75 in the UK, proved to be the last studio album The Tourists released, before the band split. A compilation, *SHOULD HAVE BEEN GREATEST HITS*, followed in 1984 but it wasn't a hit anywhere.

2 ~ SWEET DREAMS (ARE MADE OF THIS) by Eurythmics

Love Is A Stranger/I've Got An Angel/Wrap It Up/I Could Give You (A Mirror)/The Walk/ Sweet Dreams (Are Made Of This)/Jennifer/This Is The House/Somebody Told Me/This City Never Sleeps

Produced by Adam Williams, David A. Stewart & Robert Crash.

UK: RCA RCALP 6063 (1983).

12.02.83: 77-50-32-15-6-5-**3**-5-5-5-5-5-6-5-8-14-19-18-18-24-26-26-30-19-16-18-18-21-19-18-22-26-29-47-53-66-73-80-92-73-85-78-52-86-97-x-x-x-96-68-40-41-36-42-64-66-59-62-94-81-x-90-x-x-97-94
15.06.91: 64

Australia
9.05.83: peaked at no.**5**, charted for 32 weeks

Canada
2.07.83: 90-84-81-62-57-53-36-26-20-16-11-9-**6-6-6-6-6-6-6**-9-9-11-13-16-22-24-26-26-26-28-34-37-40-37-40-37-43-43-51-55-55-59-59-60-70-74-76-76-78

Germany
16.05.83: 10-**6**-7-**6-6**-7-8-11-11-14-14-14-17-21-24-27-20-40-40-58-53-62

Japan
21.08.83: peaked at no.**77**, charted for 2 weeks (LP chart)

EURYTHMICS

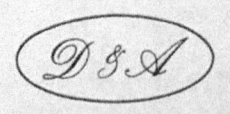

D & A

March

- 3rd   MANCHESTER Hacienda
- 4th   NOTTINGHAM Trent Polytechnic
- 5th   LOUGHBOROUGH University
- 7th   HATFIELD Polytechnic
- 8th   PORTSMOUTH Polytechnic
- 9th   SOUTHAMPTON University
- 10th   BOURNEMOUTH Academy
- 11th   SWANSEA University
- 12th   NORWICH University of East Anglia
- 13th   LONDON Lyceum

SWEET DREAMS
=are made of this·»

includes
LOVE IS A STRANGER
THE WALK

Album and Cassette

RCA

Netherlands
9.04.83: 4-33-24-22-20-24-24-20-15-21-13-14-15-21-16-13-24-15-18-**11**-18-**11**-14-26-34-36-33-50

New Zealand
26.06.83: 17-5-4-4-3-**2-2**-3-**2**-5-6-4-4-7-8-12-12-11-18-15-21-8-22-37-40-42-42-42-42-42-42-35-47-30-39-44-47-x-x-x-x-5-45-48-48

South Africa
25.06.83: peaked at no.**14**, charted for 3 weeks

Spain
14.11.83: peaked at no.**12**, charted for 12 weeks

Sweden
8.02.83: 27-30-26-**14**-21-27-33-46-30-40-45   (bi-weekly)

USA
25.06.83: 65-60-48-35-31-24-20-18-17-**15-15-15**-26-23-23-23-25-23-23-38-49-50-48-46-63-62-78-78-86-84-90-93-89-100-97-93-89-84-82-81-75-85-91-90-90-93

Zimbabwe
25.09.83: peaked at no.**4**

IN THE GARDEN, the debut album by Eurythmics, was released in October 1981 but it wasn't a hit.

Originally, Annie and Dave Stewart planned to title their second album 'Invisible Hands', after one of the tracks they recorded for the album. But, as *Invisible Hands* failed to make the final cut, they decided to go with *SWEET DREAMS (ARE MADE OF THIS)* instead, after a track that did make the album's final track listing.

The album featured a cover of *Wrap It Up*, which Sam & Dave released as the B-side of their 1968 single, *I Thank You*. On the Eurythmics version, Annie duetted with Scritti Politti's Green Gartside.

'Our philosophy about cover versions,' said Annie, 'is that if you're going to do one, then do something original with it. I wouldn't want to do a lukewarm version of an original. We take a song and explode it, rather than just doing a replica like a cabaret band would.'

This City Never Sleeps, the track that closes the album, was inspired by the time Annie spent in a small bedsit in London, after she left the Royal Academy of Music. '*This City Never Sleeps* is simply to do with what was happening to me at the time,' she said. 'You know, the walls were so thin that I could hear the girl coughing next door. It was very depressing.'

Four singles were released from *SWEET DREAMS (ARE MADE OF THIS)*, but the first two ~ *This Is The House* and *The Walk* ~ both failed to chart.

The third single, *Love Is A Stranger*, was only a minor hit first time around, and it wasn't until the album's title cut was released as the fourth and final single that Eurythmics found success, with both *Sweet Dreams (Are Made Of This)* and its parent album.

SWEET DREAMS (ARE MADE OF THIS) achieved no.2 in New Zealand, no.3 in the UK, no.4 in Zimbabwe, no.5 in Australia, no.6 in Canada and Sweden, no.11 in the Netherlands, no.12 in Spain, no.14 in South Africa and Sweden, and no.15 in the USA.

Following the success of *Sweet Dreams (Are Made Of This)*, *Love Is A Stranger* was reissued, and found success in most countries second time around.

Overall, Annie was very happy with the album.

'All the tracks are strong,' she said. 'I can put my hand on my heart and say, "I really love every track on the album". We rejected an awful lot of material and made sure there was no filler. All tuna, no celery. They're all quite different, and yet the Eurythmics sound is there.'

A similarly titled video album was also released, featuring live in-concert footage filmed at London's Heaven nightclub, plus three music videos: *Love Is A Stranger*, *Sweet Dreams (Are Made Of This)* and *Who's That Girl?*

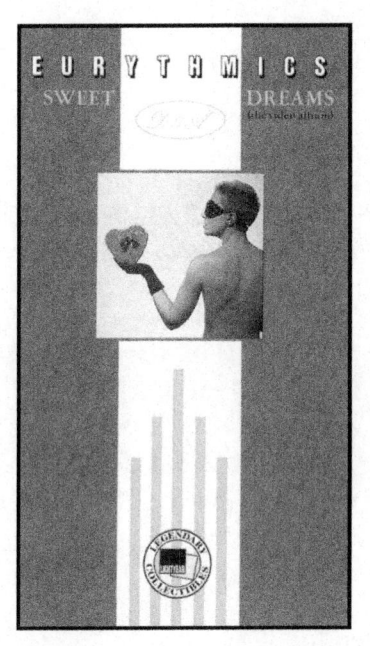

Deluxe Edition

SWEET DREAMS (ARE MADE OF THIS) was remastered and reissued in 2005, with six bonus tracks:

> Home Is Where The Heart Is/Monkey Monkey/Baby's Gone Blue/Sweet Dreams (Are Made Of This) (Hot Remix)/Love Is A Stanger (Coldcut Remix)/Satellite Of Love

3 ~ TOUCH by Eurythmics

Here Comes The Rain Again/Regrets/Right By Your Side/Cool Blue/Who's That Girl?/The First Cut/Aqua/No Fear, No Hate, No Pain (No Broken Hearts)/Paint A Rumour

Produced by David A. Stewart.

UK: RCA PL 70109 (1983).

26.11.83: 8-11-13-12-12-12-15-9-6-5-**1-1**-2-5-4-6-8-12-15-13-17-18-23-21-26-39-35-39-45-59-75-70-70-55-93-67-67-74-76-77-82-84-85-x-76-x-80-x-92-98
12.01.85: 80

Australia
19.12.83: peaked at no.**4**, charted for 37 weeks

Canada
14.01.84: 79-52-37-25-15-7-4-4-5-**3-3-3**-4-4-4-5-6-8-10-12-11-10-10-10-15-15-18-19-21-21-22-23-23-24-24-25-29-29-31-31-44-47-60-68

Germany
26.12.83: 62-61-59-46-28-16-12-**9**-15-16-20-22-22-23-26-28-27-37-46-59

Japan
21.01.84: peaked at no.**71**, charted for 3 weeks (LP chart)

152

Netherlands
26.11.83: 34-15-27-30-27-35-32-46-33-42-34-30-14-11-13-**9**-14-18-19-27-33-29-33-34-42-33-x-48-37-x-43-42

New Zealand
18.12.83: 45-45-45-45-45-2-**1**-3-3-4-4-7-9-11-7-7-5-8-8-8-10-13-26-19-17-27-24-44-42-47-47

Norway
24.12.83: 14-14-14-17-x-x-x-17-18-19-14-11-11-**8**-17-17-17-17-17

South Africa
17.03.84: peaked at no.**11**, charted for 11 weeks

Sweden
29.11.83: 23-14-10-10-12-34-35-15-**9**-19-26-45 (bi-weekly)

Switzerland
18.03.84: **14**-17-20-21-22-28-28-27-28

USA
4.02.84: 55-26-20-17-15-13-11-9-8-**7-7-7**-9-11-11-15-16-16-22-26-33-32-36-40-41-45-51-
58-62-62-75-74-75-85

Zimbabwe
1.04.84: peaked at no.**3**

TOUCH was recorded and mixed in just three weeks, at Annie and Dave Stewart's The Church studio in London.

'We started to write songs ridiculously quickly,' said Dave, 'like, people would go and get a sandwich, and come back and we'd written a song!'

'What we were striving for,' said Annie, 'is a cross between gut level feeling and intellect ~ pop music that is saying something, but is not so intellectual that you have to join a cult to understand it, something that's wonderfully functional and slithers between the extremes.'

At the same time, as Dave confirmed, the duo were keen to move on from *SWEET DREAMS (ARE MADE OF THIS)*.

'The last thing we wanted to do was to make another *SWEET DREAMS*,' he said. 'In fact, we just forgot about that completely and went in to make a record as though we'd never made one before … often, before, we'd found that an original demo is a hundred times better than the final master, it's got that initial spontaneity.'

THE FACE No. 42 — OCTOBER 1983 75p

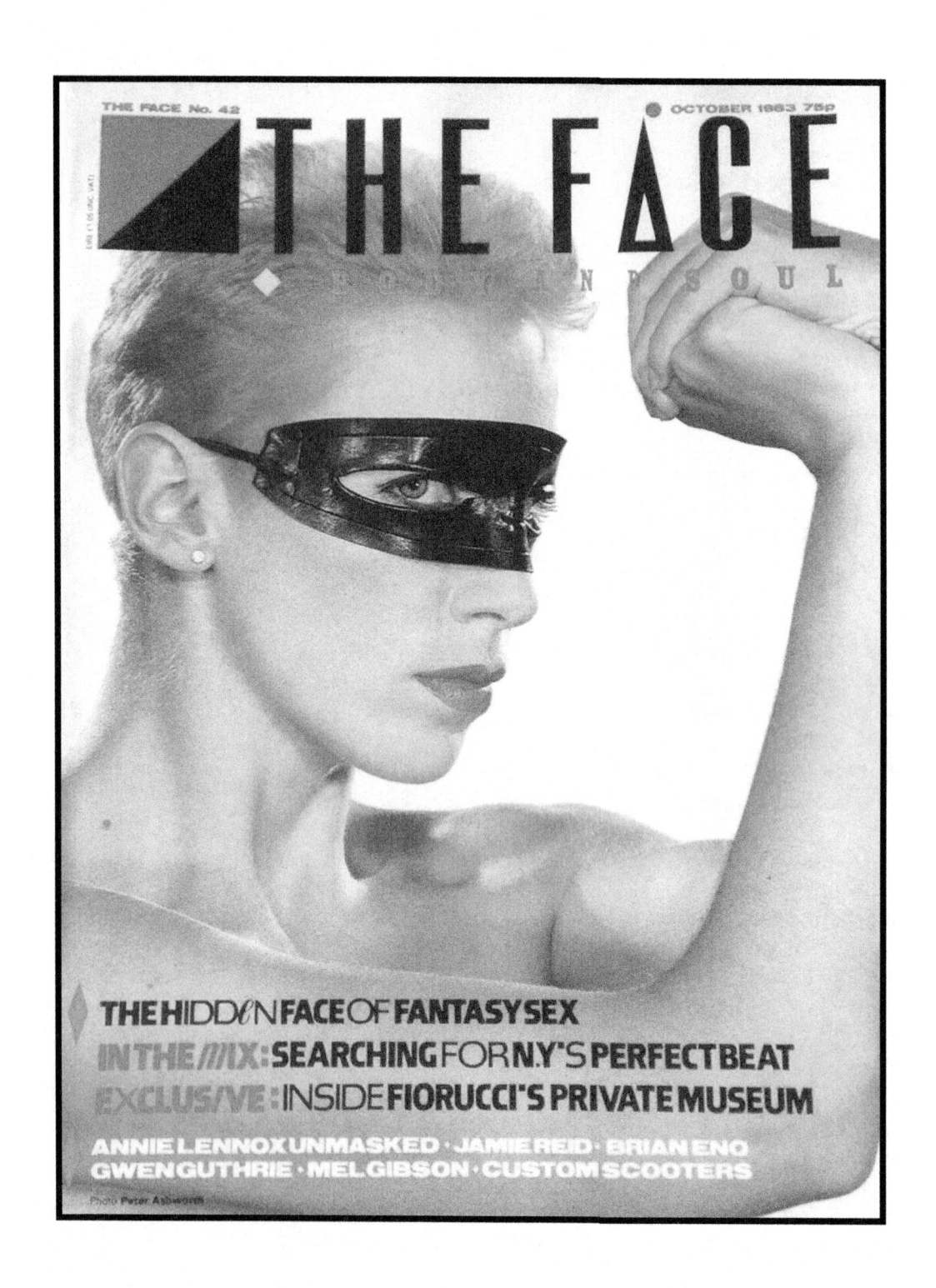

THE FACE
BODY AND SOUL

THE HIDDEN FACE OF FANTASY SEX
IN THE MIX: SEARCHING FOR N.Y.'S PERFECT BEAT
EXCLUSIVE: INSIDE FIORUCCI'S PRIVATE MUSEUM

ANNIE LENNOX UNMASKED · JAMIE REID · BRIAN ENO
GWEN GUTHRIE · MEL GIBSON · CUSTOM SCOOTERS

Photo Peter Ashworth

The album's striking sleeve was an outtake from a photo shoot that Annie did for *The Face* magazine, which took place at Bagley's warehouse with photographer Peter Ashworth.

Three hit singles were lifted from *TOUCH*:

- *Who's That Girl?*
- *Right By Your Side*
- *Here Comes The Rain Again*

TOUCH gave Eurythmics their first no.1 album in the UK It also hit no.1 in New Zealand, and achieved no.3 in Canada and Zimbabwe, no.4 in Australia, no.7 in the USA, no.8 in Norway, no.9 in Germany, the Netherlands and Sweden, no.11 in South Africa and no.14 in Switzerland.

Deluxe Edition

TOUCH was remastered and reissued in 2005 with seven bonus tracks:

You Take Some Lentils ... And You Take Some Rice/ABC (Freeform)/Plus Something Else/Paint A Rumour (Long Version)/Who's That Girl? (Live)/Here Comes The Rain Again (Live)/Fame

The last track on the deluxe edition was a cover of David Bowie's 1975 hit, *Fame*.

4 ~ TOUCH DANCE by Eurythmics

The First Cut (Vocal Remix)/Cool Blue (Vocal Remix)/Paint A Rumour (Vocal Remix)/ Regrets (Vocal Remix)/The First Cut (Instrumental Remix)/Cool Blue (Instrumental Remix)/Paint A Rumour (Instrumental Remix)

UK: RCA PG 70354 (1984).

9.06.84: **31**-33-49-36-57

This remix album featured four tracks from the Eurythmics's *TOUCH* album, plus three instrumentals, all remixed by either John 'Jellybean' Benitez and Francois Kevorkian.

Although initially open to the idea of a remix album, neither Annie or Dave Stewart had any input to *TOUCH DANCE*, and neither was happy with the final outcome and refused to endorse or promote it.

'When I say I can't stand it,' said Dave, 'I can't stand the principle of it. It's songs that I've already recorded and mixed to the best of my ability. I don't think people juggling around with the sound of things makes them any better as songs. It was some bright spark's idea, it definitely wasn't our idea.'

TOUCH DANCE made its chart debut at no.31 in the UK, but it rose no higher. Elsewhere, the album registered at no.115 on the Billboard 200 in the United States, but it failed to chart anywhere else.

5 ~ 1984 (FOR THE LOVE OF BIG BROTHER) by Eurythmics

I Did It Just The Same/Sexcrime (Nineteen Eighty-Four)/For The Love Of Big Brother/ Winston's Diary/Greetings From A Dead Man/Julia/Doubleplusgood/Ministry Of Love/ Room 101

Produced by David A. Stewart.

UK: Virgin V1984 (1984).

24.11.84: 27-27-29-30-36-36-31-28-25-25-**23**-26-44-59-64-84-90

Australia
14.01.85: peaked at no.**22**, charted for 13 weeks

Canada
8.12.84: 79-69-55-55-48-42-40-40-40-38-37-34-34-**33-33**-37-53-63-67-69

Germany
17.12.84: 41-37-37-27-24-26-**23**-29-36-42-37-46-64

Japan
1.02.85: peaked at no.**51**, charted for 5 weeks (LP chart)

Netherlands
15.12.84: 49-49-44-43-**38**-42-42

THE FACE No. 57
THE FACE
1984
WRIT LARGE
BEST, WORST, UPS, DOWNS; ALL THE ANGLES ON '84
ANNIE LENNOX FACE INTERVIEW
SPITTING IMAGES
PAUL YOUNG
DAN AYKROYD
HEALTH CLUB DISCOS
JAMES TRUMAN NY 84

New Zealand
10.03.85: 31-28-24-**21**-24-24-26-40-47

Sweden
7.12.84: 38-24-19-11-**6**-7-18-35 (bi-weekly)

Switzerland
20.01.85: 26-**18**-21-20-26

USA
2.02.85: 100-98-98-**93**

1984 was a 1984 film based on George Orwell's classic 1949 novel with the same title. The film starred Richard Burton, John Hurt and Suzanna Hamilton, and was directed by Michael Radford.

Virgin Films, who financed the project, approached Annie and Dave Stewart, to ask them if they would compose the film's soundtrack.

'We turned it down,' said Dave. 'It's taken us this long to get our songwriting together. At the moment, we just want to make great Eurythmics records. A lot of people tend to jump into all things when they get famous and spread themselves really thinly. I mean, we'd never written a soundtrack!'

But, following repeated requests, Annie and Dave finally changed their minds.

'I was really worried about doing it,' said Annie, "cos I actually thought I couldn't take it. After all, I'm not the cheeriest of chapesses.'

Deadlines were tight and, after agreeing to go ahead, Annie and Dave composed and recorded the music for the film in just seven days, and completed the soundtrack album in 20 days.

But no-one thought to inform the film's director Michael Radford about Annie and Dave's involvement. 'I knew (Richard) Branson was looking,' he said, 'but it was far too late. He never told me he had hired Eurythmics.'

Pushed for time, Radford commissioned Dominic Muldowney to compose an orchestral soundtrack for *1984*.

Radford was furious when he found out about Eurythmics' involvement; he wasn't a fan of their music, and he didn't want their music in his film.

'I asked Branson,' he said, 'what legally was the minimum amount of music I could put on the movie to allow him to put out a record. He said fifteen seconds, so I put fifteen seconds of their music on the film.'

Annie and Dave only found out their music hadn't been used at the film's premiere.

Not happy with how *1984* was doing at the box office, Virgin Films took the unusual decision to pull the film from cinemas, and re-release it with the Eurythmics soundtrack accounting for 95% of the film's music ~ a decision that infuriated director Michael Radford, but saw box office taking significantly increase.

GEORGE ORWELL'S TERRIFYING VISION COMES TO THE SCREEN.
1984
JOHN HURT RICHARD BURTON
in Michael Radford's film of George Orwell's "NINETEEN EIGHTY-FOUR"
with SUZANNA HAMILTON CYRIL CUSACK
A Virgin Films/Umbrella-Rosenblum Films Production Director of Photography ROGER DEAKINS
Editor TOM PRIESTLEY Production Designer ALLAN CAMERON Music by EURYTHMICS & DOMINIC MULDOWNEY
Executive Producer MARVIN J. ROSENBLUM Co-Producers AL CLARK & ROBERT DEVEREUX Produced by SIMON PERRY
Written and Directed by MICHAEL RADFORD FROM ATLANTIC RELEASING CORP. ©1984
Title Theme "Sexcrime – 1984" performed by Eurythmics
Original Soundtrack on RCA Records and Cassettes

Not wanting to get involved in all the acrimony, Annie retreated to her home in Switzerland. 'We wash our hands of it,' she said. 'We did what we were asked to do, we made a soundtrack and an album that we both feel really proud of. But at this moment I'm so fed up with people saying one thing, and doing another, that I really couldn't care less.'

The soundtrack album, *1984 (FOR THE LOVE OF BIG BROTHER)*, gave Eurythmics two hit singles:

- *Sexcrime (Nineteen Eighty-Four)*
- *Julia*

While it couldn't match the success of *TOUCH*, *1984 (FOR THE LOVE OF BIG BROTHER)*, was reasonably successful in many countries. It achieved no.6 in Sweden, no.18 in Switzerland, no.21 in New Zealand, no.22 in Australia, no.23 in Germany and the UK, no.33 in Canada, no.38 in the Netherlands and no.51 in Japan. In the United States, where *Sexcrime (Nineteen Eighty-Four)* was effectively banned, the album struggled to no.93.

Today, two versions of *1984* are available: a version featuring music by Eurythmics, and a director's cut featuring the orchestral soundtrack composed by Dominic Muldowney.

6 ~ BE YOURSELF TONIGHT by Eurythmics

Would I Lie To You?/There Must Be An Angel (Playing With My Heart)/I Love You Like A Ball And Chain/Sisters Are Doin' It For Themselves/Conditioned Soul/Adrian/It's Alright (Baby's Coming Back)/Here Comes That Sinking Feeling/Better To Have Lost In Love (Than Never To Have Loved At All)

Produced by David A. Stewart.

UK: RCA PL 70711 (1985).

11.05.85: 4-**3**-6-8-10-12-20-28-22-14-5-**3-3-3**-5-8-8-13-19-20-25-32-42-49-50-56-49-38-
52-60-61-57-67-66-57-34-21-12-7-7-7-**3**-5-5-7-8-10-12-14-17-23-26-28-31-40-49-47-
47-38-47-53-55-47-62-59-54-63-69-69-69-74-78-71-70-79-88-x-99
3.01.87: 94-82
28.02.87: 75

Australia
3.06.85: peaked at no.**1** (4), charted for 54 weeks

Austria
1.10.85: **25** (bi-weekly)

Canada
18.05.85: 70-39-31-20-11-4-**3-3-3**-5-6-6-11-11-10-10-10-12-12-11-10-11-11-12-13-18-
23-28-30-30-30-37-37-45-45-45-47-47-46-45-48-54-63-63-66-73-81-97

EURYTHMICS

BE YOURSELF TONIGHT

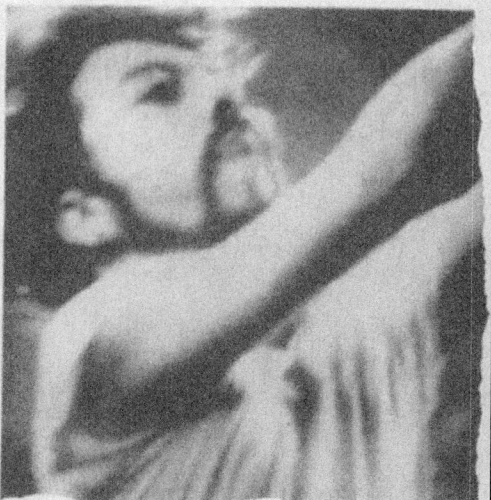

THE NEW ALBUM & CHROME CASSETTE
(COMING SOON ON CD)

includes

WOULD I LIE TO YOU?

produced by David A. Stewart

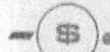

RCA

Finland
06.85: peaked at no.**3**, charted for 21 weeks

France
2.06.85: **20** (monthly)

Germany
20.05.85: 29-24-24-20-12-16-16-21-21-28-25-24-18-15-10-9-9-**8**-11-14-15-17-24-29-35-40-46-52-56-61-51-60-60

Japan
5.06.85: peaked at no.**44**, charted for 6 weeks (LP chart)

Netherlands
18.05.85: 10-12-9-10-12-17-23-31-43-x-44-8-13-7-**3**-5-4-7-7-8-13-21-25-29-44-44-46-52-48-39-46-52
1.02.86: 40-11-11-14-17-20-24-29-30-27-42-47-61-75

New Zealand
7.07.85: 12-4-5-8-13-14-11-10-5-5-4-**2**-7-7-8-8-10-10-13-12-15-28-26-29-29-29-29-29-26-30-26-33-39-42-40-41-8-19-27-27-27-22-24-23-27-48-50

Norway
18.05.85: 11-11-7-6-8-10-9-12-16-12-13-x-**2**-**2**-**2**-**2**-**2**-**2**-5-4-6-6-8-18-18-16-20

South Africa
12.10.85: peaked at no.**4**, charted for 17 weeks

Spain
28.10.85: peaked at no.**18**, charted for 11 weeks

Sweden
17.05.85: 3-**2**-**2**-3-3-3-**2**-**2**-**2**-4-5-11-23-34-38-45-x-37-x-44 (bi-weekly)

Switzerland
12.05.85: 30-24-**9**-10-11-14-17-20-25-24-x-30-x-30-23-20-19-19-23-30-23-29

USA
25.05.85: 52-37-29-18-14-12-10-10-**9**-14-14-13-14-14-12-14-13-16-19-24-26-31-33-33-36-41-43-52-56-64-64-78-78-81-91-98

Zimbabwe
25.08.85: peaked at no.**3**

Following the difficulties that plagued the *1984 (FOR THE LOVE OF BIG BROTHER)* soundtrack, Annie and Dave Stewart were keen to move on, and put the whole episode behind them.

'I've already an idea what our next Eurythmics LP is going to be musically,' said Dave, 'lots more real instruments. An Eastern feel mixed with the heart of soul music. We're going to get a double-decker bus with a studio and drive off to France or Spain ~ it reminds me of *Summer Holiday*!'

Between *TOUCH* and the album that became *BE YOURSELF TONIGHT*, Annie had married and divorced, and this attracted a lot of media attention.

'I'm not somebody who wished to draw attention to my romantic life or my emotions,' she said. 'It's been difficult, because at the same time that (the divorce) was announced, so was our album, so the papers wanted to write about me and my divorce instead.'

Annie and Dave composed all the songs for *BE YOURSELF TONIGHT*, which was recorded in Paris, Detroit and Los Angeles, and mixed in Los Angeles. Unusually for Eurythmics, the album featured high profile guest appearances from Aretha Franklin (on *Sisters Are Doin' It For Themselves*), Stevie Wonder (on *There Must Be An Angel (Playing With My Heart)*) and Elvis Costello (on *Adrian*).

'I have a deep respect for Elvis,' said Annie. 'and a great deal of admiration because he's, mainly for me, an extraordinary lyricist ... he's a very intense person and I like people like that. I like people who put their beliefs on the line when they write a song.'

BE YOURSELF TONIGHT yielded four hit singles:

- *Would I Lie To You?*
- *There Must Be An Angel (Playing With My Heart)*
- *Sisters Are Doin' It For Themselves*
- *It's Alright (Baby's Coming Back)*

The album hit no.1 in Australia, and charted at no.2 in New Zealand, Norway and Sweden, no.3 in Canada, Finland, the Netherlands, the UK and Zimbabwe, no.4 in South Africa, no.8 in Germany, no.9 in Switzerland and the USA, no.18 in Spain, no.20 in France, no.25 in Austria and no.44 in Japan.

Deluxe Edition

BE YOURSELF TONIGHT was remastered and reissued in 2005, with six bonus tracks:

Grown Up Girls/Tous Les Garcons Et Les Filles/Sisters Are Doin' It For Themselves (ET Mix)/Would I Lie To You? (ET Mix)/Conditional Soul (Live)/Hello, I Love You

The closing bonus track, *Hello, I Love You*, was written by Jim Morrison, and was originally recorded by The Doors for their 1968 album, *WAITING FOR THE SUN*. Released as a single, *Hello, I Love You* went to no.1 in both Canada and the United States.

7 ~ REVENGE by Eurythmics

Missionary Man/Thorn In My Side/When Tomorrow Comes/The Last Time/The Miracle Of Love/Let's Go/Take Your Pain Away/A Little Of You/In This Town/I Remember You

Produced by David A. Stewart.

UK: RCA PL 71050 (1986).

12.07.86: **3-3**-4-5-5-7-12-7-9-7-**3**-4-**3**-5-6-5-10-9-13-18-18-18-16-13-9-8-10-9-14-15-18-20-16-14-12-16-20-26-27-29-45-46-46-54-56-60-75-83-100-97-98-x-x-96

Australia
14.07.86: peaked at no.**2**, charted for 58 weeks

Austria
15.08.86: 17-13-10-9-**6**-10-14-12-10-15-16-22-19-25-25-25-25-28 (bi-weekly)

Canada
5.07.86: 83-74-57-42-28-13-10-7-4-4-**3**-4-4-4-5-5-6-12-12-10-13-?-17-19-26-26-26-26-27-27-25-27-29-35-35-38-42-42-46-64-64-82-100

Finland
07.86: peaked at no.**1** (2), charted for 37 weeks

France
6.12.86: 13-18-**12**-16 (monthly)

EURYTHMICS
Revenge. A game two can play.
"REVENGE" includes the hits:
"MISSIONARY MAN"
"WHEN TOMORROW COMES"
"THORN IN MY SIDE"
Produced by David A. Stewart
RCA
Records, Cassettes and Compact Discs
REVENGE

Germany
14.07.86: 27-14-10-8-8-7-6-8-9-12-13-14-7-**5**-7-7-9-11-14-15-18-16-16-21-21-24-28-30-36-35-36-42-46-52-59-62-62-63

Japan
21.07.86: peaked at no.**46**, charted for 5 weeks (LP chart)

Netherlands
12.07.86: 14-**3**-**3**-5-**3**-6-12-11-10-16-26-30-34-37-46-49-55-45-50-49-51-49-45-47-46-54-40-47-55-69

New Zealand
10.08.86: 9-5-2-2-2-2-4-5-8-7-14-12-6-11-10-8-11-10-9-9-9-9-9-**1-1-1-1-1-1-1-1-1-1**-3-5-7-7-7-11-18-17-21-29-23-37-31-35-48

Norway
12.07.86: 6-**1-1-1-1-1-1-1**-2-2-2-3-5-5-5-6-5-4-4-4-3-5-5-5-6-6-6-6-6-7-9-12-11-14-15-20

South Africa
26.10.86: peaked at no.**17**, charted for 3 weeks

Spain
15.09.86: peaked at no.**17**, charted for 16 weeks

Sweden
9.07.86: **1-1-1-1-1-1**-2-2-3-5-6-10-17-32 (bi-weekly)

Switzerland
13.07.86: 13-8-9-**7**-10-**7**-9-10-11-13-14-11-11-**7**-8-10-12-8-11-**7**-9-16-19-15-21-17-19-13-13-13-20-28-20-30

USA
9.08.86: 52-29-22-18-16-15-14-14-**12**-15-18-21-24-27-30-33-41-42-52-66-79-79-79-81

Following a battle against stomach cancer, Annie's father Tom Lennox died on 8th April 1986.
 'When someone is dying you long to do something,' said Annie. 'He suffered so much, *so much*. You're standing on the sidelines and there's this hopeless, helpless feeling … It's a very strange feeling seeing that fragility, that vulnerability, thinking, "That's my father dying".'
 Her father's passing inspired two of the songs Eurythmics recorded for their new album, *REVENGE*, *I Remember You* and *Take Your Pain Away*. Incredibly, Annie and

Dave Stewart composed all the songs for the album in just one week, and recorded the album ~ in Paris and Cologne, Germany ~ in under a month.

'It's frightening because it's so intense and argumentative,' said Dave. 'I even add pressure by saying that we have to make the album in three weeks or whatever. Annie will ask why and I'll make up some lame excuse, but really it's because I like that kind of pressure to make things work.'

'Dave is a facilitator,' said Annie. 'Very often he captures an idea as it comes from me and takes it several steps further. Then I take the idea a few steps further still, and we swap back and forth until the song is done. It's funny, we don't talk a lot during this process. I've developed a wonderful appreciation for it over time.'

Unlike *BE YOURSELF TONIGHT*, there were no high profile guests on *REVENGE*; this was a conscious decision.

'We had guests on *BE YOURSELF TONIGHT*,' said Annie, 'but we haven't done the same thing on this album because we never like to retread what we've done before. We wanted to show Eurythmics as being a live band, sounding like a live band, a real unit.'

Four hit singles were released from *REVENGE*:

- *When Tomorrow Comes*
- *Thorn In My Side*
- *The Miracle Of Love*
- *Missionary Man*

REVENGE went all the way to no.1 in Finland, New Zealand, Norway and Sweden, and achieved no.2 in Australia, no.3 in Canada, the Netherlands and the UK, no.5 in Germany, no.6 in Austria, no.7 in Switzerland, no.12 in France and the USA, no.17 in South Africa and Spain, and no.46 in Japan.

Deluxe Edition

REVENGE was remastered and reissued in 2005, with six bonus tracks:

When Tomorrow Comes (Extended Version)/Thorn In My Side (Extended Version)/ Missionary Man (Extended Version)/When Tomorrow Comes (Live Acoustic Version)/ Revenge 2/My Guy

Revenge 2 was a radical remake of *Revenge*, a track Annie and Dave recorded for the first Eurythmics album, *IN THE GARDEN*.

My Guy was written ~ as *My Girl* ~ by Smokey Robinson and Ronald White, and was originally recorded by The Temptations in 1964. The Temptations took *My Girl* to no.1 in the United States.

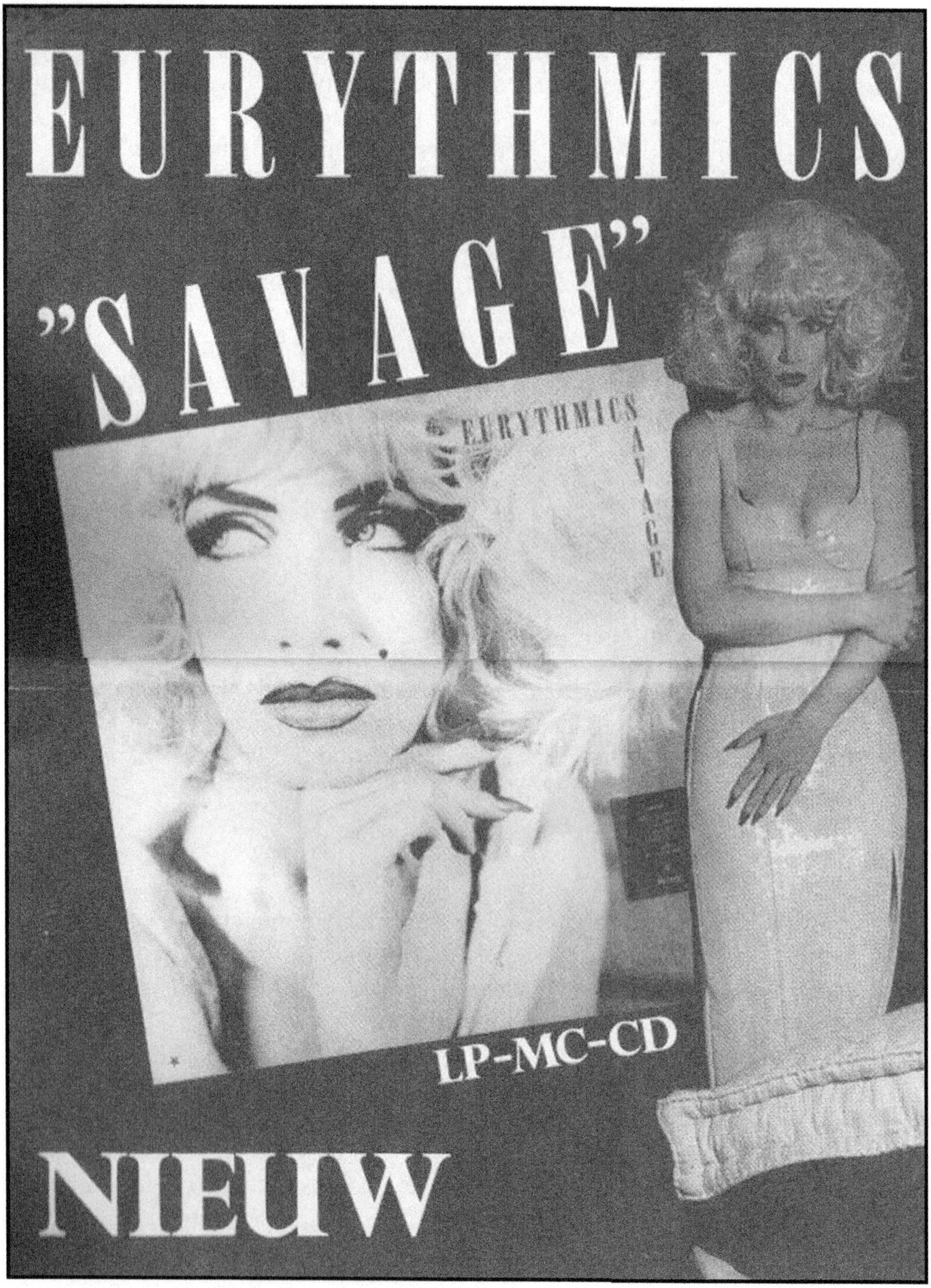
EURYTHMICS
"SAVAGE"
EURYTHMICS
SAVAGE
LP-MC-CD
NIEUW

8 ~ SAVAGE by Eurythmics

Beethoven (I Love To Listen To)/I've Got A Lover (Back In Japan)/Do You Want To Break Up?/You Have Placed A Chill In My Heart/Shame/Savage/I Need A Man/Put The Blame On Me/Heaven/Wide Eyed Girl/I Need You/Brand New Day

Produced by David A. Stewart.

UK: RCA PL 71555 (1987).

21.11.87: **7**-13-25-33-36-36-32-33-36-43-42-60-66-77
9.04.88: 76-56-50-74-89-x-x-x-x-73-56-33-28-28-32-40-40-40-41-50-62-83-75

Australia
14.12.87: peaked at no.**15**, charted for 23 weeks

Austria
15.12.87: 24-x-**17** (bi-weekly)

Canada
12.12.87: 72-50-34-34-34-19-12-**9**-10-**9**-**9**-14-14-15-17-25-28-28-29-31-38-38-44-52-61-74-76-80-86-93-100

Finland
11.87: peaked at no.**12**, charted for 10 weeks

France
22.11.87: **26**-27 (bi-weekly)

Germany
23.11.87: 50-50-**23**-26-27-27-35-43-40-46-50-52-52-63

Japan
25.12.87: peaked at no.**77**, charted for 3 weeks (LP chart)

Netherlands
28.11.87: **26-26**-42-55-69-x-57-58-58-68

New Zealand
20.12.87: 39-39-39-39-15-20-13-**7**-12-16-10-22-19-23-29-28-28-21-19-20-33-32-32-33-46

Norway
21.11.87: 15-**10**-13-11-17

Sweden
25.11.87: **2**-7-12-15-26-45 (bi-weekly)

Switzerland
29.11.87: 28-**10**-15-21-26

USA
9.01.88: 92-61-51-46-**41-41**-53-58-66-76-93-95

Zimbabwe
10.04.88: peaked at no.**10**

'When I wrote songs for our new album *SAVAGE*,' said Annie, 'I had just broken up with the man I had been living with for two years and it left me reeling. I wasn't prepared for it and I felt very betrayed. It was as if my world was caving in on me.'

Dave Stewart described *SAVAGE* as an 'annihilation album'.

'A lot of Annie's words were about the despair and pain of being on the receiving end of men being so horrible,' he said. 'That was Annie's time-out, it was almost a solo album except that I made the music with her.'

SAVAGE was recorded at Chateau Dangu, Paris, where Dave had married Bananarama's Siobhan Fahey ~ who was expecting his child ~ on 1st August 1987. Unusually, Dave recorded the music for the album without Annie being there.

'Annie came in twice in three months,' he revealed, 'because she was so fucked up. She'd just split up with somebody. I made the whole album virtually on my own. Then I met Annie in Paris and we were great friends again, and she did the vocals in a week ~ just poured it out.'

'There's a depth to it we haven't touched before,' said Annie. 'It's dark and I like the sharpness of its blade.'

SAVAGE produced four hit singles:

- *Beethoven (I Love To Listen To)*
- *Shame*
- *I Need A Man*
- *You Have Placed A Chill In My Heart*

Although not as successful as the two previous Eurythmics albums, *SAVAGE* achieved no.2 in Sweden, no.7 in New Zealand and the UK, no.9 in Canada, no.10 in Norway and Switzerland, no.12 in Finland, no.15 in Australia, no.17 in Austria, no.23 in Germany, no.26 in France and the Netherlands, and no.41 in the USA.

Deluxe Edition

SAVAGE was remastered and reissued in 2005, with five bonus tracks:

Beethoven (I Love To Listen To) (Extended Philharmonic Version)/Shame (Dance Mix)/
I Need A Man (Macho Mix)/I Need You (Live)/Come Together

Come Together was composed by John Lennon & Paul McCartney, and was originally recorded by The Beatles for their 1969 album, *ABBEY ROAD*. Released as a double A-side with *Something*, The Beatles took *Come Together* to no.1 in the United States and no.4 in the UK.

Eurythmics
WE TWO ARE
ONE TOO /Video

WORLDWIDE RELEASE 23rd APRIL 1990   CATALOGUE No: 790 349

9 ~ WE TOO ARE ONE by Eurythmics

We Too Are One/The King And Queen Of America/(My My) Baby's Gonna Cry/Don't Ask Me Why/Angel/Revival/You Hurt Me (And I Hate You)/Sylvia/How Long?/When The Day Goes Down

Produced by David A. Stewart & Jimmy Iovine.

UK: RCA PL 74251 (1989).

23.09.89: **1**-2-4-8-8-17-19-19-17-22-24-29-34-41-39-41-44-34-38-37-28-27-29-25-31-39-49-55-60-75
26.05.90: 73-69

Australia
25.09.89: peaked at no.**8**, charted for 29 weeks

Austria
1.10.89: 30-**20**-27 (bi-weekly)

Canada
18.09.89: 89-21-18-18-17-17-17-16-15-**12**-16-14-16-13-13-13-13-18-18-34-28-29-42-32-29-33-51-57-67-74-69-66-67-70-71-91

Finland
09.89: peaked at no.**9**, charted for 10 weeks

France
8.10.89: **11**-13-14-21-19-33-45 (bi-weekly)

Germany
25.09.89: 10-10-**4**-**4**-6-10-12-18-21-27-30-38-34-43-43-47-51-49-63-58-55-62-59-58-56-64-66-61-62-74-69-72-76-82

Japan
11.09.89: peaked at no.**38**, charted for 5 weeks (CD chart)

Netherlands
30.09.89: 51-29-21-**18**-29-38-52-65-77-85

New Zealand
22.10.89: 10-17-12-**8**-15-20-30-41

Norway
23.09.89: 6-4-**3**-**3**-5-5-8

South Africa
12.10.89: peaked at no.**4**, charted for 13 weeks

Spain
2.10.89: peaked at no.**29**, charted for 13 weeks

Sweden
20.09.89: **1**-2-2-4-6-22-49-37-27 (bi-weekly)

Switzerland
24.09.89: **2**-3-**2**-3-4-6-7-8-11-14-21-23-30

USA
7.10.89: 51-46-44-44-44-41-**34**-**34**-37-38-35-36-36-37-39-46-48-53-65-77-83-88-95

WE TOO ARE ONE, the title of what proved to be the last Eurythmics album of new songs for a decade, raised a few eyebrows.

'It's like a statement,' said Dave Stewart. 'We've been through all this and we're still as strong as ever, with the same kind of vision.'

Annie chose to interpret the album's title differently, stating that it referred to her relationship with her new husband Uri Fruchtmann, who she had married in Paris on 15th July 1988. 'Uri is my refuge,' she said. 'My rock. It's about time I had a relationship that works.'

WE TOO ARE ONE took Annie and Dave five weeks to record in mid-1989 ~ however, where possible, they opted to work on the album separately. The album attracted mixed reviews, and yielded four Top 40 singles:

- *Revival*
- *Don't Ask Me Why*
- *The King And Queen Of America*
- *Angel*

A fifth single, *(My My) Baby's Gonna Cry* was released in North America only, thus becoming the first Eurythmics singles to not be issued in the UK. It was a minor hit in Canada, but failed to enter Billboard's Hot 100 in the United States.

WE TOO ARE ONE made its chart debut in the UK at no.1, to give Eurythmics their second chart topper, after *TOUCH*. The album also went to no.1 in Sweden, and charted at no.2 in Switzerland, no.3 in Norway, no.4 in Germany and South Africa, no.8 in Australia and New Zealand, no.9 in Finland, no.11 in France, no.12 in Canada, no.18 in the Netherlands, no.20 in Austria, no.29 in Spain, no.34 in the USA and no.38 in Japan.

Deluxe Edition

WE TOO ARE ONE was remastered and reissued in 2005, with five bonus tracks:
Precious/See No Evil/The King And Queen Of America (Dance Remix)/Angel (Choir Version)/Last Night I Dreamt That Somebody Loved Me

Last Night I Dreamt That Somebody Loved Me was written by Morrissey and Johnny Marr, and was originally recorded by The Smiths for their 1987 album, *STRANGEWAYS, HERE WE COME*. The track was released as a single in the UK, with a photograph of a young Billy Fury on the sleeve; it charted at no.30.

On 18th February 1990, Annie picked up her fourth BRIT Award, for Best British Female Solo Artist. During her acceptance speech, she surprised everyone by announcing that she would be giving up her career, so she could concentrate on having a family and working for the homeless charity, Shelter.

'We'd been through such a lot,' she later explained, 'and never had a break, like a divorced couple that want to be apart. Wanting to make music was what kept us together, but now we need space if we're not going to destroy the goodwill that exists between us. It's a very strange relationship, but then, it always has been.'

Dave Stewart understood and supported Annie's viewpoint. He said, 'It got to the point where if one of us walked into a room and the other was in there, you'd want to walk out. We came to the sad realisation that we had to get away or we would destroy each other.'

10 ~ GREATEST HITS by Eurythmics

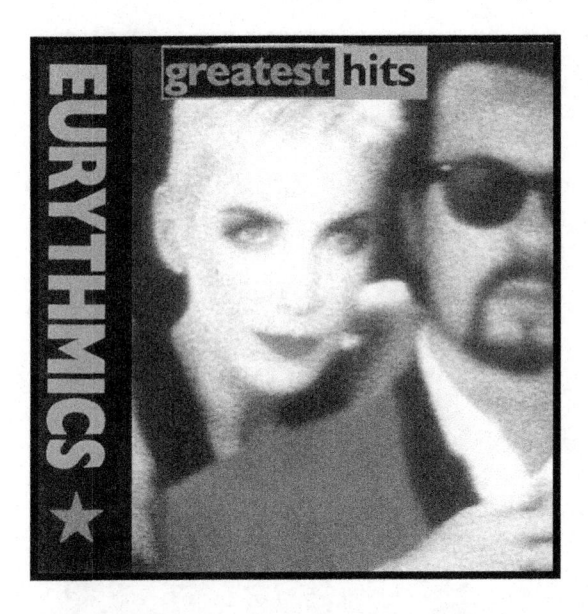

Love Is A Stranger/Sweet Dreams (Are Made Of This)/Who's That Girl?/Right By Your Side/Here Comes The Rain Again/There Must Be An Angel (Playing With Your Heart)/Sisters Are Doin' It For Themselves/It's Alright (Baby's Coming Back)/When Tomorrow Comes/You Have Placed A Chill In My Heart/The Miracle Of Love/Sexcrime (Nineteen Eighty-Four)/Thorn In My Side/Don't Ask Me Why/Angel/Would I Lie To You?/Missionary Man/I Need A Man

UK: RCA PD 74856 (1991).

30.03.91: **1-1-1-1-1-1-1-1-1**-2-4-4-**1**-3-3-6-7-9-6-7-8-11-13-11-14-14-13-17-20-27-32-35-36-38-31-26-30-33-35-34-27-27-28-30-35-37-38-39-42-53-52-48-52-62-59-61-61-60-64-60-67-53-55-68-62-61-63-x-62-60-68-72-x-73-70-50-53-72-90-81-90-85-68-68-74-80-89-x-61-50-55-56-48-55-75-93-88-91-81-81-89
10.04.93: 66-50-46-51-65-83-x-x-x-87-85-99-x-x-x-94
1.01.94: 97-x-x-x-x-92
20.02.99: 64-11-15-20-26-36-51-89
8.01.00: 55-88-52-79-27-23-45-46-50-80-90-90-x-x-x-83-45-50-50-61-21-43-71-x-x-x-x-x-85-x-x-x-x-x-x-x-73-78-50-69-75-79
6.01.01: 26-35-43-72-x-x-x-99-75-73
9.06.01: 98-83
16.07.05: 68-78-78-90-x-x-86

Australia
1.04.91: peaked at no.**1** (6), charted for 46 weeks

179

greatest hits
EURYTHMICS
INCLUDES THE HITS
SWEET DREAMS (Are Made Of This)
HERE COMES THE RAIN AGAIN
WOULD I LIE TO YOU?
MISSIONARY MAN
PLUS 10 MORE OF THEIR
ALL-TIME BEST
THE ALBUM. THE HOME VIDEO.

Austria
14.04.91: 17-2-2-2-**1-1**-2-2-2-2-2-2-2-10-7-7-7-8-5-10-10-12-10-14-17-17

Canada
15.06.91: 42-14-12-**10**-12-12-14-15-11-14-17-19-17-23-23-24-26-30-44-48-54-63-64-62-68-68-83-86-86-86-86-94-95

Finland
03.91: peaked at no.**4**, charted for 17 weeks

France
26.04.91: 2-**1-1**-2-3 (bi-weekly)
22.04.01: 28-34

Germany
1.04.91: 43-16-**1**-2-2-2-2-2-2-2-2-2-2-2-3-4-4-6-6-7-7-8-9-12-11-16-19-24-28-30-34-32-30-34-32-30-35-36-44-50-58-54-54-55-61-57-56-65-58-59-62-65-69-76-76
8.11.99: 57-100

Japan
21.03.91: peaked at no.**63**, charted for 6 weeks (CD chart)

Netherlands
30.03.91: 69-15-6-3-2-**1-1-1-1-1-1**-2-5-8-9-7-6-6-11-11-12-12-12-15-16-20-32-40-63-72-66-59-58-57-60-82
22.04.00: 95-98

New Zealand
14.04.91: 6-**1-1-1-1-1-1-1-1**-3-4-3-4-7-10-12-13-19-20-14-15-20-14-18-35-41-43

Norway
30.03.91: 16-16-7-**5-5**-8-8-14-16-20
1.05.99: 16-15-25-34-40
14.08.99: 30-x-x-x-31-39
27.01.01: 40-38
26.01.02: 33
22.06.02: 40

South Africa
4.05.91: peaked at no.**2**, charted for 27 weeks

Spain
8.04.91: peaked at no.**4**, charted for 30 weeks

Sweden
27.03.91: 30-10-**8**-11-11-13-16-39-34-x-50-x-25 (bi-weekly)

Switzerland
31.03.91: 10-9-3-3-**2**-3-3-3-4-4-11-10-14-13-20-24-20-12-19-19-24-19-28-26

USA
29.06.91: 84-77-78-78-**72**-78-88-89-85-90-95-100

With Annie and Dave Stewart having agreed to split, and go their separate ways, a Eurythmics greatest hits compilation was almost inevitable.

GREATEST HITS spanned the years 1982-90, and featured most of the duo's biggest hits though, curiously, *Beethoven (I Love To Listen To)* was omitted. The international edition of the compilation featured 18 hits, however, in North America a 14-track version was released which saw *Right By Your Side*, *Sexcrime (Nineteen Eighty-Four)*, *It's Alright (Baby's Coming Back)*, *You Have Placed A Chill In My Heart* and *The Miracle Of Love* all dropped, and *The King And Queen Of America* added.

The track listing of the North American release was as follows:

Sweet Dreams (Are Made Of This) (12" Version)/When Tomorrow Comes (LP Version)/Here Comes The Rain Again (12" Version)/Who's That Girl? (Short Version)/Would I Lie To You? (LP Version)/Sisters Are Doin' It For Themselves (LP Version)/There Must Be An Angel (Playing With My Heart) (LP Version)/Missionary Man (7" Version)/Don't Ask Me Why (Short LP Version)/I Need A Man (LP Version)/Love Is A Stranger (LP Version)/Thorn In My Side (LP Version)/The King And Queen Of America (LP Version)/Angel (Greatest Hits Edit)

GREATEST HITS was hugely successful in most countries, and became Annie and Dave's best-selling album globally.

In the UK, *GREATEST HITS* stormed to no.1 ~ a position it held for nine straight weeks, and in total it topped the chart for 10 non-consecutive weeks. The compilation also hit no.1 in Australia, Austria, France, Germany, the Netherlands and New Zealand, and charted at no.2 in South Africa and Switzerland, no.4 in Finland and Spain, no.5 in Norway, no.8 in Sweden and no.10 in Canada.

11 ~ DIVA

Why/Walking On Broken Glass/Precious/Legend In My Living Room/Cold/Money Can't Buy It/Little Bird/Primitive/Stay By Me/The Gift

CD Bonus Track: *Keep Young And Beautiful*

Japan & Mexico Bonus Track: *Step By Step*

Produced by Stephen Lipson.

UK: RCA PD 75326 (1992).

18.04.92: **1**-2-3-2-4-7-6-8-12-9-11-15-23-24-30-24-22-21-14-8-6-5-6-6-9-11-12-13-14-16-15-18-20-17-18-17-19-17-22-24-31-29-25-20-11-3-**1**-6-6-8-7-7-6-8-15-17-14-25-30-30-36-37-39-51-55-56-59-67-65-70-82-71-84-98-98
5.02.94: 82
18.03.95: 32-35-52-68-70
29.07.95: 82-91
2.03.96: 77-55-54-69-95
8.06.96: 64-81-95
19.10.96: 97-90-98
1.03.97: 97

Australia
10.05.92: **7**-14-12-18-21-28-29-22-24-17-40-28-36-x-x-x-x-48-33-36-33-34-37-44-41-48-49-49-43

31.01.93: 50

Austria
19.04.92: 30-34-**3**-8-13-15-9-19-18-18-25-21-24-21-25-28

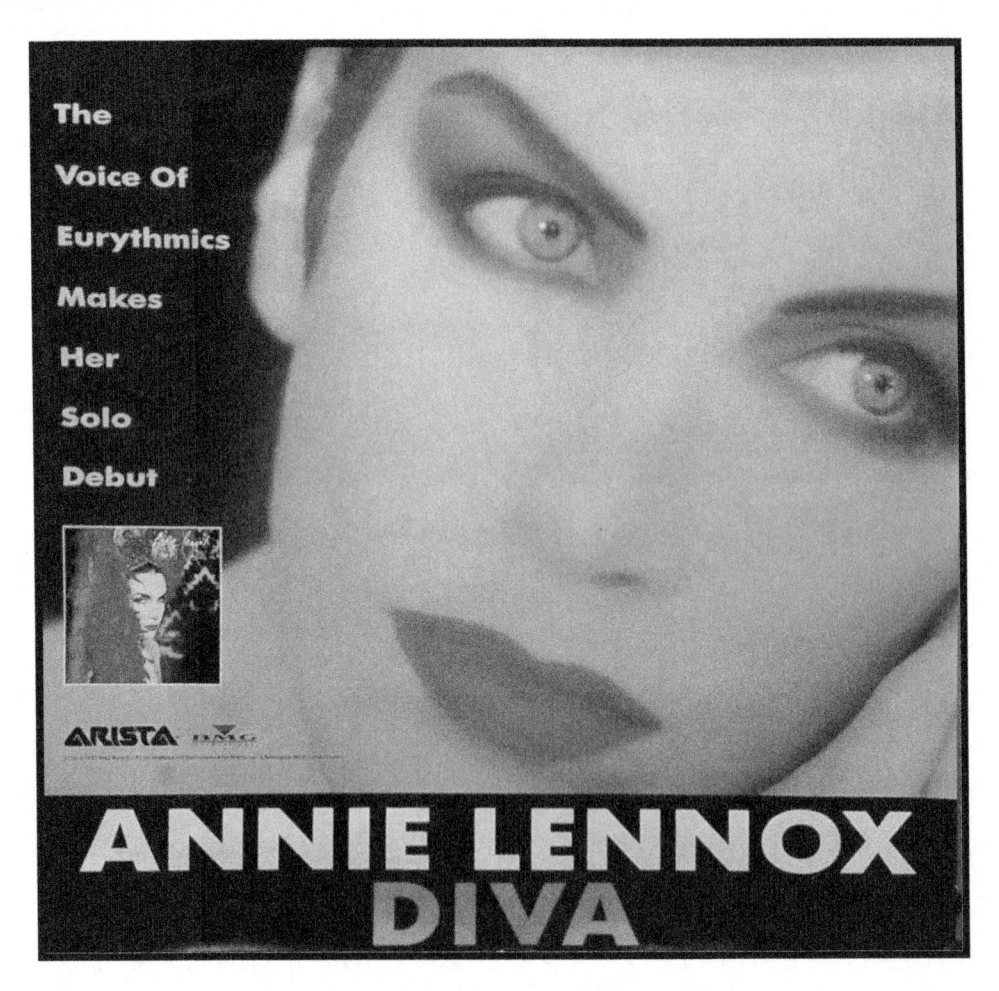

Canada
9.05.92: 31-17-**6-6**-8-9-8-10-11-11-9-8-9-12-17-21-22-25-31-29-28-28-26-27-24-26-23-29-26-26-28-30-28-25-25-25-22-20-18-22-20-20-17-24-25-24-26-27-30-31-31-35-46-46-56-57-52-55-62-79-81-85-83-83

Finland
04.94: peaked at no.**18**, charted for 17 weeks

France
6.05.92: **48** (bi-weekly)

184

Germany
20.04.92: 38-24-**6**-8-7-7-**6**-7-12-13-19-19-23-24-26-30-33-36-34-28-24-24-26-29-33-33-36-35-40-43-48-52-59-62-67-60-60

Netherlands
18.04.92: 74-30-16-13-8-6-**5**-9-10-13-17-24-40-41-41-48-69-78-84-87-92-77-68-x-96-96

New Zealand
10.05.92: 15-13-**6**-8-9-11-10-12-18-25-40-49
25.10.92: 22-24-23-16-19-14-29-26-34-34-34-34-39-43-44

Norway
2.05.92: **11**-12-14

South Africa
16.05.92: peaked at no.**12**, charted for 9 weeks

Spain
18.05.92: peaked at no.**36**, charted for 12 weeks

Sweden
15.04.92: 10-8-8-**5**-**5**-6-6-10-14-15-28-29 (bi-weekly)

Switzerland
19.04.92: 30-12-8-6-7-**5**-8-6-9-12-12-15-16-18-20-21-20-22-27-28-35-40

USA
30.05.92: 33-32-29-28-27-28-33-39-32-31-**23**-29-32-34-34-34-36-30-31-33-38-35-33-35-33-37-38-45-51-53-53-52-48-49-45-39-32-34-34-29-31-23-29-42-48-50-53-62-70-79-79-81-91-98

Annie recorded her first solo album at two London studios, The Church and Mayfair Studios.

'The cover is a photograph by a young Japanese artist who lives and works in Paris,' said Annie, 'he's called Satoshi ... we did this in very early December of last year and I didn't have a title for the album. In January, the prints of the session came to me in Los Angeles, and when I looked at these prints and I knew mentally the list of titles I had conjectured for the album, I knew exactly then what the title had to be.'

That title was *DIVA*.

'It's meant to be partly ironic,' said Annie. 'My life is divided into the public me and the private me. In the public me, I am seen as a woman on a pedestal, an artifice, who glides from place to place, a grandiose figure with no other life. That's the one I'm projecting. It's not me, of course. It's myth-making, the lifestyle of the persona I'm creating.'

Annie wrote eight of the ten tracks on *DIVA* herself, and co-wrote the other two, *Legend In My Living Room* and *The Gift*. Five hit singles were released from the album:

- *Why*
- *Precious*
- *Walking On Broken Glass*
- *Cold*
- *Little Bird*

DIVA made its chart debut in the UK at no.1, and achieved no.3 in Austria, no.5 in the Netherlands, Sweden and Switzerland, no.6 in Canada, Germany and New Zealand, no.7 in Australia, no.11 in Norway, no.12 in South Africa, no.18 in Finland, no.23 in the USA, no.36 in Spain and no.48 in France.

At the same time as the album, Annie released a *Diva* video album, featuring seven promos plus an excerpt from a previously unreleased song, *Remember*. The featured videos were as follows:

Why/Legend In My Living Room/Money Can't Buy It/Cold/Remember (Excerpt)/ Primitive/The Gift/Keep Young And Beautiful

The home video was reissued later in the year, re-titled *Totally Diva*, with two promos added, *Precious* and *Walking On Broken Glass*.

At the 1993 BRIT awards, Annie won Album of the Year for *DIVA*. She also picked up a Grammy nomination, again for Album of the Year, in the United States, but she lost out to Eric Clapton's *UNPLUGGED*. She did, however, win a Grammy Award for the home video *Diva*, for Best Music Video, Long Form.

12 ~ LIVE 1983-1989 by Eurythmics

CD1:
Never Gonna Cry Again (recorded at The Hacienda, Manchester, on 3rd March 1983)
Love Is A Stranger (Six Flags Magic Mountain, Los Angeles, 20th August 1983)
Sweet Dreams (Are Made Of This) (Quartier Latin, Berlin, 22nd March 1983)
This City Never Sleeps (Apollo, Manchester, 6th November 1983)
Somebody Told Me (The Buffalo, New York City, 1st April 1984)
Who's That Girl? (Auditorium, Chicago, 5th April 1984)
Right By Your Side (Austin, Texas, April 1984)
Here Comes The Rain Again (Johanneshovs Isstadion, Stockholm, 3rd October 1986)
Sexcrime (Nineteen Eighty-Four) (Stadthalle, Fürth, Germany, 28th October 1986).
I Love You Like A Ball And Chain (Palazzo dello Sport, Rome, 31st October 1986)
Would I Lie To You? (Southern Star Amphitheater, Houston, Texas, 16th August 1986)

CD2:
There Must Be An Angel (Playing With My Heart) (Wembley Arena, London, December 1986)
Thorn In My Side (Brighton Centre, Brighton, 12th December 1986)
Let's Go (Town Hall, Christchurch, 24th January 1987)
Missionary Man (Entertainment Centre, Sydney, 14th February 1987)
The Last Time (Entertainment Centre, Melbourne, 7th March 1987)
The Miracle Of Love (Entertainment Centre, Sydney, 14th February 1987)
I Need A Man (Palazzo dello Sport, Rome, 27th October 1989)
We Too Are One (Point Theatre, Dublin, 8th September 1989)
(My My) Baby's Gonna Cry (Playhouse, Edinburgh, 11th September 1989)

Don't Ask Me Why (Palazzo dello Sport, Rome, 27th October 1989)
Angel (Wembley Arena, London, 23rd September 1989)

Note: *The Miracle Of Love* was incorrectly credited as being recorded in Paris.

CD3 (Limited Edition Bonus Acoustic CD):
You Have Placed A Chill In My Heart/Here Comes The Rain Again/Would I Lie To You?/ It's Alright (Baby's Coming Back)/Right By Your Side/When Tomorrow Comes

All the tracks on CD3 were recorded at Rome's Palazzo dello Sport on 27th October 1989.

Produced by David A. Stewart.

UK: RCA 74321177042 (1993).

27.11.93: **22**-32-36-50-56-66-84
17.06.95: 51

Austria
26.12.93: **40**

Germany
10.01.94: 100-**80**-83-87-81-98-98

Netherlands
4.12.93: 90-82-**80**-94

This live compilation of hits was recorded at various venues around the world between March 1983 and October 1989.

LIVE 1983-1989 fared best in the UK, where it achieved no.22. The live set also charted at no.40 in Austria, and was a minor hit in Germany and the Netherlands, but it failed to chart in most countries.

Reissued in 1995, *LIVE 1983-1989* returned to the UK chart for one week at no.51.

13 ~ MEDUSA

No More "I Love You's"/Take Me To The River/A Whiter Shade Of Pale/Don't Let It Get You Down/Train In Vain/I Can't Get Next To You/Downtown Lights/Thin Line Between Love And Hate/Waiting In Vain/Something So Right

Japan Bonus Track: *Heaven*

Limited Edition Bonus CD: *Live In Central Park: Money Can't Buy It/Legend In My Living Room/Who's That Girl?/You Have Placed A Chill In My Heart/Little Bird/ Walking On Broken Glass/Here Comes The Rain Again/Why/Something So Right (Studio Version featuring Paul Simon)*

Produced by Stephen Lipson.

UK: RCA 74321257172 (1995).

18.03.95: **1**-2-2-4-3-6-6-6-10-12-10-13-13-8-10-10-12-15-18-24-33-38-31-37-41-49-46-52-41-45-30-31-46-58-71-87-97-92-84-44-42-39-37-36-38-45-53-70-74-69-56-59-70-81

Australia
19.03.95: **5**-7-7-12-21-24-33-37-36-36

Austria
19.03.95: 6-5-**2**-4-5-6-9-11-10-16-14-18-27-32-30-33

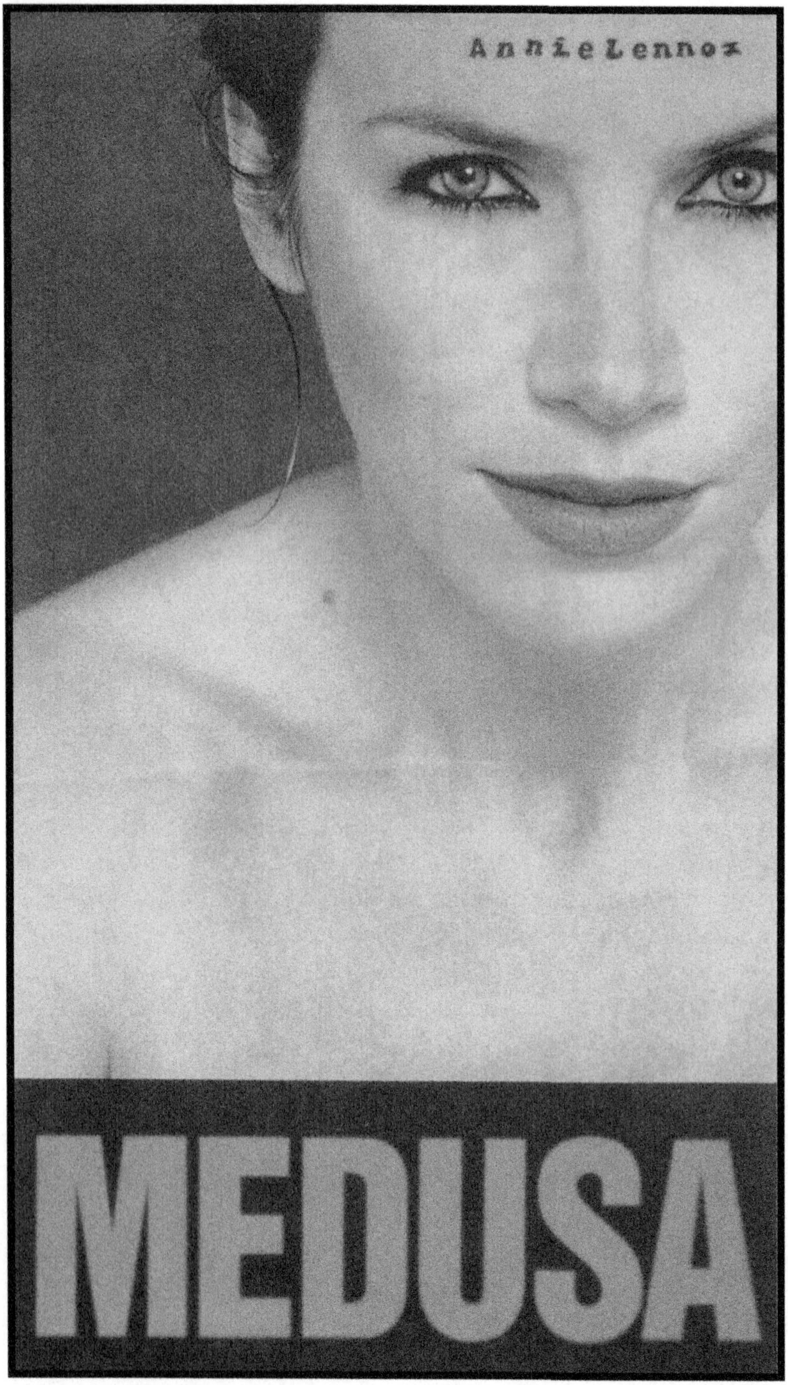
AnnieLennox
MEDUSA

Belgium
1.04.95: 10-**8**-10-12-15-22-26-28-28-25-38-38-32-50-44-x-48-46

Canada
27.03.95: 2-2-2-2-**1**-2-2-3-4-3-3-5-6-9-11-11-14-19-19-19-22-23-17-8-8-10-12-16-18-24-35-46-55-64-70-79-85-90-90-90-90-90-92-92-82-82-92

Finland
03.95: peaked at no.**10**, charted for 10 weeks

France
5.03.95: **5**-8-14-17-19-19-15-18-24-22-38-48-41-25-39-42-46

Germany
20.03.95: 22-11-**4-4**-5-**4**-6-9-11-12-12-14-17-19-26-29-37-35-34-39-50-48-56-54-71

Netherlands
18.03.95: 35-15-**7-7**-9-15-26-26-36-43-60-62-71-73-76-68-53-41-39-40-54-54-68-73-85-98-100

New Zealand
16.04.95: 11-6-**5**-7-6-8-7-7-7-12-22-31-38-46-50

Norway
11.03.95: 20-**4**-5-6-7-6-8-13-13-18-18-25-21-32-34-26-32-36-33-x-x-x-36

Spain
6.03.95: peaked at no.**5**, charted for 2 weeks

Sweden
17.03.95: 5-**4**-12-13-18-16-21-14-21-22-25-23-19-31-28-25-26-33-27-28-28-36-31-32-42-48-37-42-49-x-x-x-50-46

Switzerland
19.03.95: 11-21-**6-6-6-6**-9-10-9-14-11-15-20-23-33-35-46-47-x-43

USA
1.04.95: **11**-12-17-18-19-21-20-20-19-19-17-21-24-26-29-30-32-36-41-40-43-42-43-39-41-37-43-42-57-83-92-99
16.03.96: 75-93

Zimbabwe
21.08.95: peaked at no.**6**

Unlike her first album, *DIVA*, Annie's second was an album entirely of cover versions.

'It has arisen from the need to do something different,' Annie explained. 'To qualify that, from the early Eighties I have been writing and co-writing songs, and arrived at the stage where I just wanted to break the pattern for a while.'

Annie, unusually for her, knew what the album's title was going to be even before she started work on it.

'When I wrote songs with Dave and then subsequently with *DIVA*, there was a title that emerged from the songs. It came right at the very end of the whole process, always, but in this case I had this name sitting around even before the album was put into production, and I liked it. I liked all the implications of it.'

The title she chose was *MEDUSA*.

In Greek mythology, Medusa was a Gorgon ~ a winged human female with venomous snakes instead of hair, who turned anyone who looked at her to stone.

As well as vocals, Annie also played most of the keyboards parts on the album, and devised the arrangements with producer Stephen Lipson. The album was recorded at The Aquarium studios, London, between January and May 1994.

In the album's liner notes, Annie wrote:

'This album contains a selection of songs I have been drawn to for all kinds of reasons. They were not chosen with any particular theme or concept in mind ~ the method was more by instinct than design. The work undertaken was truly a labour of love for me and I feel privileged to have been given this opportunity.'

Four singles were released from *MEDUSA*:

- *No More "I Love You's"*
- *A Whiter Shade Of Pale*
- *Waiting In Vain*
- *Something So Right*

Like *DIVA* before it, *MEDUSA* stormed straight to no.1 in the UK. It also topped the Canadian album chart, and achieved no.2 in Austria, no.4 in Germany, Norway and Sweden, no.5 in Australia, France, New Zealand and Spain, no.6 in Switzerland and Zimbabwe, no.7 in the Netherlands, no.8 in Belgium, no.10 in Finland and no.11 in the USA.

14 ~ PEACE by Eurythmics

17 Again/I Saved The World Today/Power To The Meek/Beautiful Child/Anything But Strong/Peace Is Just A Word/I've Tried Everything/I Want It All/My True Love/Forever/ Lifted

Produced by Andy Wright & Eurythmics.

UK: RCA 74321695622 (1999).

30.10.99: **4**-9-24-34-42-45-51-50-50-52-70-42-30-28-21-28-37-48-62-89
27.05.00: 72

Australia
31.10.99: 10-**8**-18-29

Austria
30.10.99: 9-8-**7**-10-15-22-35-41-47-47-47

Belgium
23.10.99: 41-10-**9**-20-25-46

Canada
25.10.99: 57-20-**9**-18-37-37-49-61-59-46-46-46-36-36-50-47-68-87-92-100

Finland
16.10.99: 33-**22**-28-**22**-27-39

France
17.10.99: **6**-8-11-14-27-35-45-56-61-65-69-70

Germany
1.11.99: **2**-4-6-10-13-14-19-24-31-31-35-29-38-36-38-57-51-66-79-98-91

Japan
27.10.99: **62** (CD chart)

Netherlands
23.10.99: 48-25-**22**-25-45-63-78-81-80-86-95-98-99

Norway
23.10.99: **22**-29-32

Spain
18.10.99: peaked at no.**32**, charted for 2 weeks

Sweden
28.10.99: **5**-9-12-18-38-44-36-41-40-40-45-52

Switzerland
31.10.99: **2**-2-3-5-9-15-28-39-53-75-69-81-90-75-72-85

USA
6.11.99: **25**-47-75-79-98

Annie and Dave Stewart reunited in the first half of 1998, to play two one-off concerts. Working together on new material wasn't on the agenda, but they surprised themselves by writing 4-5 new songs in as many days.

'It's been so long,' said Dave, 'that we actually forgot how good it was to write songs together and play together. We had a great time playing the songs. It's a great feeling.'

'After we'd written about six or seven songs,' said Annie, 'we thought, "Are we making an album?" We didn't tell the record company what we were doing because we didn't want to make it a big issue.'

The album was recorded during 1998-99 at London's The Church studio, and was mixed at Whitfield Street Studios, also in the capital. The title *PEACE* was chosen to reflect Annie and Dave's ongoing concerns regarding global conflict and world peace.

The Eurythmics premiered the songs from *PEACE* with a concert aboard *Rainbow Warrior II*, a Greenpeace ship, and followed this with a 24-date world 'Peacetour'. Annie and Dave agreed all proceeds from the album and tour would be split 50-50 between Greenpeace and the human rights organisation, Amnesty International.

EURYTHMICS
THE NEW ALBUM Peace
Annie Lennox. Dave Stewart.
Together Again.
Sweet Dreams
Do Come True!
Annie
Dave
sam goody
www.arista.com
www.peacetour.net
ARISTA
BMG
© 1999 BMG Entertainment International, UK and Ireland Ltd.
Photography: ANOUSHKA FISZ

OUT NOW ON DVD VIDEO
EURYTHMICS peacetour
'IF ONLY ALL MUSIC DVD's WERE LIKE THIS'
TOTAL DVD
Annie...
...Dave
www.click2music.co.uk
THE ULTIMATE EURYTHMICS EXPERIENCE FEATURING ALL THE CLASSIC HITS
EXTRAS ON DVD INCLUDE: BONUS 60 MIN. DOCUMENTARY 'PEACETALK'
MULTI-ANGLE TRACKS, FULLY INTERACTIVE DISCOGRAPHY,
PICTURE GALLERY, WEBLINKS, LYRICS & DOLBY DIGITAL 5.1 OPTION
OUT NOW TO BUY ON DVD & VHS 3rd JULY AT WOOLWORTHS

'We want to strengthen the membership of the organisations,' said Annie, 'because it's only with strong membership that they can be really effective. So we're trying to do that, trying to raise the profile. It was a kind of campaigning run, as well as a concert tour.'

The final date of the Peacetour on 6th December 1999, staged at London Docklands Arena, was filmed and released as a home video/DVD. It featured:

I Want It All/Missionary Man/Thorn In My Side/When Tomorrow Comes/It's Alright (Baby's Coming Back)/I Saved The World Today/Who's That Girl?/I Love You Like A Ball And Chain/Would I Lie To You?/Sisters Are Doin' It For Themselves/17 Again/ You Have Placed A Chill In My Heart/Love Is A Stranger/I Need A Man/Walking On Broken Glass/There Must Be An Angel (Playing With My Heart)/Here Comes The Rain Again/Why/The Miracle Of Love/Peace Is Just A Word/Sweet Dreams (Are Made Of This)

PEACE achieved no.2 in Germany and Switzerland, no.4 in the UK, no.5 in Sweden, no.6 in France, no.7 in Austria, no.8 in Australia, no.9 in Belgium and Canada, no.22 in Finland, the Netherlands and Norway, no.25 in the USA and no.32 in Spain.

Two hit singles were released from *PEACE*:

- *I Saved The World Today*
- *17 Again*

A third single, *Peace Is Just A Word*, was issued in the UK and Europe, but it wasn't a hit.

Deluxe Edition

PEACE was remastered and reissued in 2005, with four bonus tracks:

Beautiful Child (Acoustic Version)/17 Again (Acoustic Version)/I Saved The World Today (Acoustic Version)/Something In The Air

Something In The Air was written by Speedy Keen, and was originally recorded by Thunderclap Newman for their 1969 album, *HOLLYWOOD DREAM*. Thunderclap Newman took *Something In The Air* all the way to no.1 in the UK.

15 ~ BARE

A Thousand Beautiful Things/Pavement Cracks/The Hurting Time/Honestly/Wonderful/ Bitter Pill/Loneliness/The Saddest Song I've Got/Erased/Twisted/Oh God (Prayer)

Japan Bonus Track: *Cold (Live)*

Limited Edition Bonus DVD: *A Thousand Beautiful Things (Live)/Wonderful (Live)/ Interview*

Produced by Amy Wright, Annie Lennox & Stephen Lipson.

UK: RCA/BMG/19 Recordings 8287652248-2 (2003).

21.06.03: **3**-5-10-18-32-44-50-55-57-73-71-76-x-x-x-57-63-60-76-93

Australia
22.06.03: **10**-12-22-37-55-58-37-52-62-62-96

Austria
22.06.03: 20-**17**-29-30-49-53-61-62-71

Belgium
28.06.03: **20**-46-45

France
8.06.03: **34**-48-73-85-93-86

Germany
23.06.03: **5**-6-10-17-23-24-29-38-46-52-70-86

Netherlands
21.06.03: 26-24-33-37-33-29-19-**18-18**-23-29-43-58-79-93

New Zealand
13.07.03: **20**-25-26-25-28-31-31-41-42

Norway
21.06.03: **16**-26-39

Sweden
19.06.03: **29**-30-46-57

Switzerland
22.06.03: 9-**7**-10-15-20-25-24-31-43-42-55-75

USA
28.06.03: **4**-5-10-14-18-25-34-35-38-50-66-65-73-87

Following an album of covers versions, Annie returned to song-writing, and she penned all the tracks she recorded for her third solo album, *BARE*.

Unusually, Annie didn't shoot any promo videos for any of the songs on *BARE*, nor were any of the three singles that were released from the album really promoted, or given a full release; in most countries, only promos were released. The singles were:

- *Pavement Cracks*
- *A Thousand Wonderful Things*
- *Wonderful*

Pavement Cracks was given a full release in North America, while *Wonderful* was issued on 12" in the UK, but none of the three singles became hits.

The lack of hit singles and promotion meant *BARE* failed to match the success of *DIVA* and *MEDUSA*, but it still enjoyed reasonable success in many countries, charting at no.3 in the UK, no.4 in the USA, no.5 in Germany, no.7 in Switzerland, no.10 in Australia, no.16 in Norway, no.17 in Austria, no.18 in the Netherlands, no.20 in Belgium and New Zealand, no.29 in Sweden and no.34 in France.

EURYTHMICS ULTIMATE COLLECTION

THEIR GREATEST HITS DIGITALLY REMASTERED ON ONE ALBUM

07.11.05

- THORN IN MY SIDE
- SWEET DREAMS (ARE MADE OF THIS)
- WHO'S THAT GIRL?
- HERE COMES THE RAIN AGAIN
- THERE MUST BE AN ANGEL (PLAYING WITH MY HEART)
- LOVE IS A STRANGER
- RIGHT BY YOUR SIDE
- WOULD I LIE TO YOU?
- SISTERS ARE DOIN' IT FOR THEMSELVES
- IT'S ALRIGHT (BABY'S COMING BACK)
- WHEN TOMORROW COMES
- THE MIRACLE OF LOVE
- MISSIONARY MAN
- YOU HAVE PLACED A CHILL IN MY HEART
- I NEED A MAN
- I SAVED THE WORLD TODAY
- 17 AGAIN

CD INCLUDES BRAND NEW SONGS **'I'VE GOT A LIFE'** AND **'WAS IT JUST ANOTHER LOVE AFFAIR?'**

DVD FEATURES 17 ERA DEFINING VIDEOS INCLUDING THE NEW SINGLE **'I'VE GOT A LIFE'**

THE CLASSIC ALBUMS RELEASED 14th NOVEMBER 2005

- 8 Digitally Remastered Albums • Featuring Over 40 Bonus Tracks • Deluxe Packaging • Unseen Photos • New Sleeve Notes

Plus 'BOXED' - All Eight Upgraded Albums In One Limited Edition Box Set

WWW.EURYTHMICS.COM

16 ~ ULTIMATE COLLECTION by Eurythmics

I've Got A Life/Love Is A Stranger/Sweet Dreams (Are Made Of This)/Who's That Girl?/ Right By Your Side/Here Comes The Rain Again/Would I Lie To You?/There Must Be An Angel (Playing With My Heart)/Sisters Are Doin' It For Themselves/It's Alright (Baby's Coming Back)/When Tomorrow Comes/Thorn In My Side/The Miracle Of Love/Missionary Man/You Have Placed A Chill In My Heart/I Need A Man/I Saved The World Today/17 Again/Was It Just Another Love Affair?

iTunes Bonus Track: *The King And Queen Of America*

UK: RCA/Sony BMG Music 82876748412 (2005).

19.11.05: **5**-7-9-15-18-19-20-36-41-49-42-57-61-78-75-97
24.06.06: 81-82-86-78-50-56-64-77-73-77-84-89-95
21.03.09: 100-x-x-x-x-x-93-78-88-91-x-x-x-x-97-x-x-90-86-86-88-89-91
17.03.12: 88-88-92
12.05.12: 95-87

Australia
5.02.06: 21-**14**-19-22-29-34-41-47-54-71-86-87
20.06.10: 62-46-48-45-49

Austria
20.11.05: **29**-30-49-60-75
20.01.06: 72-74

203

Belgium
19.11.05: 24-13-**12**-20-29-33-40-42-46-51-55-72-79-93-92-83-95

Finland
26.11.05: **40**

France
11.11.05: **17**-20-24-40-40

Germany
18.11.05: 42-**36**-58-79

Netherlands
12.11.05: 83-44-**40**-58-67-68-71-79-75-51-46-48-52-64-87-62-67-78
22.07.06: 80-87-71-71-74

New Zealand
6.02.06: 10-10-**6**-10-10-12-17-22-25-39

Norway
26.01.08: **40**

Spain
20.11.05: 97-**68**-77

Sweden
17.11.05: 19-**14**-18-28-29-31-30-41-45-57-50-57-58-59

Switzerland
20.11.05: **24**-26-37-51-81-x-x-88

The second Eurythmics compilation shared a very similar track listing to the first, 1991's *GREATEST HITS*.

Sexcrime (Nineteen-Eighty-Four), which Annie and Dave had recorded for Virgin rather than their own record label RCA, was dropped, as were two hits from their *WE TOO ARE ONE* album, *Don't Ask Me Why* and *Angel*. Two previously unreleased songs, recorded during the *PEACE* sessions, were added, namely *I've Got A Life* and *Was It Just Another Love Affair?*, as were two hits from *PEACE*, *I Saved The World Today* and *17 Again*.

ULTIMATE COLLECTION was never going to match the enormous success of *GREATEST HITS*, but nevertheless it sold reasonably well in most countries, charting at no.5 in the UK, no.6 in New Zealand, no.12 in Belgium, no.14 in Australia and Sweden, no.17 in France, no.24 in Switzerland, no.29 in Austria, no.36 in Germany, and no.40 in Finland, the Netherlands and Norway.

One week after *ULTIMATE COLLECTION* was released, all the Eurythmics' studio albums (except *1984 (FOR THE LOVE OF BIG BROTHER)*, which had been recorded for Virgin) were remastered and reissued, each with bonus tracks. These deluxe editions were issued individually, and as a box-set titled simply *BOXED*.

17 ~ SONGS OF MASS DESTRUCTION

Dark Road/Love Is Blind/Smithereens/Ghosts In My Machine/Womankind/Through The Glass Darkly/Lost/Coloured Bedspread/Sing/Big Sky/Fingernail Moon

Barnes & Noble Bonus Tracks: *Dark Road (Acoustic Version)/Don't Take Me Down*

iTunes Bonus Tracks: *Walking On Broken Glass (Live)/Dark Road (Live)*

Bonus Tracks Edition: *Little Bird (Live)/Walking On Broken Glass (Live)/Smithereens* (with audio commentary)/*Sing* (with audio commentary)/*Dark Road* (with audio commentary)

The deluxe edition featured track-by-track commentaries, the music video for *Dark Road* and other bonus materials.

Produced by Glen Ballard.

UK: RCA/BMG/19 Recordings 88697154522 (2007).

13.10.07: **7**-18-39-67

Australia
28.10.07: **41**-61-87-81

Austria
12.10.07: **25**-36-61

Belgium
13.10.07: 59-**57**-83

France
6.10.07: **28**-42-71-94

Germany
12.10.07: 29-**15**-44-79-99

Netherlands
6.10.07: 45-**26**-60-92

Spain
7.10.07: **94**

Sweden
11.10.07: **26**-37-54

Switzerland
14.10.07: **7**-17-24-41-57

USA
20.10.07: **9**-21-28-43-63

Annie's fourth solo album was recorded at two Hollywood studios, The High Window and Westlake, between September 2006 and February 2007. Once again, she wrote all the tracks on the album herself, except *Womankind*, which she co-wrote with Nadirah X, a Jamaican poet/hip-hop artist who also featured on the track.

Annie recorded *Sing* with 23 invited female guests, including Madonna, who sang the second verse. Among the other artist who featured on the track were Anastacia, Beverley Knight, Dido, Céline Dion, Faith Hill, Gladys Knight, Joss Stone, k.d. lang, KT Tunstall, Martha Wainwright, P!nk, Shakira and Sugababes.

'Madonna is very rigorous in what she gets involved in,' said Annie, 'and for her to do that for me, I was thrilled to bits.'

Two singles were released from *SONGS OF MASS DESTRUCTION*:

- *Dark Road*
- *Sing*

Dark Road was a minor hit in Switzerland and the UK, but surprisingly, given the all-star line-up, *Sing* could only manage a lowly no.161 in the UK. It did rise to no.18 on Billboard's Dance Club Songs chart, but the single failed to enter the Top 100 of any mainstream charts anywhere.

The text on the sleeve of *Sing*, which Annie wrote, stated:

'Several years ago I personally witnessed Nelson Mandela, standing in front of his former prison cell on Robben Island, addressing the world's press. His message was that the pandemic of HIV/AIDS in Africa was in fact, a genocide. Since that time I have resolved to do as much as I can to bring attention to the HIV/AIDS crisis.'

Sing was issued as a 12" picture disc single in the UK, and Annie donated all proceeds from the song to the Treatment Action Campaign, which was set up to raise money and awareness surrounding HIV/AIDS.

SONGS OF MASS DESTRUCTION achieved no.7 in Switzerland and the UK, no.9 in the USA, no.15 in Germany, no.25 in Austria, no.26 in the Netherlands and Sweden, no.28 in France, no.41 in Australia and no.57 in Belgium.

18 ~ THE ANNIE LENNOX COLLECTION

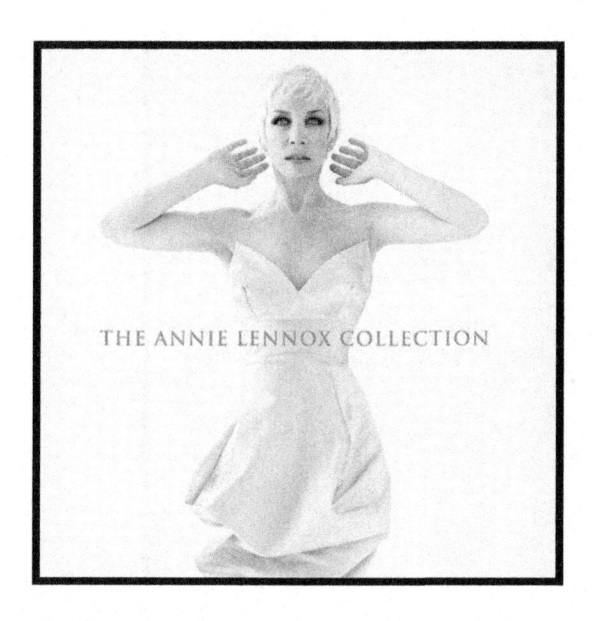

Little Bird/Walking On Broken Glass/Why/No More "I Love You's"/Precious/A Whiter Shade Of Pale/A Thousand Beautiful Things/Sing/Pavement Cracks/Love Song For A Vampire/Cold/Dark Road/Pattern Of My Life/Shining Light

CD2 (Deluxe Edition): *Into The West/Ladies Of The Canyon/Hush. Hush. Hush/Many Rivers To Cross/Dream Angus/Mama/Everybody Hurts (Live From Keep A Child Alive's Black Ball UK)/Ev'ry Time We Say Goodbye*

DVD (Deluxe Edition): *Little Bird/Walking On Broken Glass/Why/No More "I Love You's"/Precious/A Whiter Shade Of Pale/A Thousand Beautiful Things/Sing/Pavement Cracks/Cold/Dark Road/Pattern Of My Life/Shining Light/Something So Right/Waiting In Vain*

UK: RCA/Sony/19 Recordings 88697368052 (Standard Edition), 88697368082 (Deluxe Edition (2009).

21.03.09: **2-2**-5-3-4-8-9-11-16-22-31-46-65-82-95
9.01.10: 81-65-66-88-100-100-88-100
9.04.11: 34-71

Australia
12.04.09: 21-17-23-28-42-**10-10**-23-33-47-62-66-89

Austria
20.03.09: **27**-35-42-74

TWELVE LEGENDARY HITS.
TWO ELECTRIFYING BRAND NEW SONGS.
THE ANNIE LENNOX COLLECTION
TWELVE DEFINING HITS including:
"WHY," "WALKING ON BROKEN GLASS,"
"NO MORE 'I LOVE YOU'S'" and much more
PLUS
TWO NEW INSTANT CLASSICS!
Also available as a LIMITED EDITION CD & DVD
www.annielennox.com
ARISTA
IN STORES FEBRUARY 10

Belgium
21.03.09: 64-**41**-49-68-61-90-x-95

Germany
20.03.09: **15**-33-50-63-93-85-82-99

Netherlands
21.03.09: 34-**25**-28-47-51-74-76-90

New Zealand
9.03.09: 5-**4**-4-11-7-5-9-7-12-9-23-31

Norway
16.05.09: 9-**4**-5-7-10-24-29

Switzerland
22.03.09: **23**-30-49-62-79-92

USA
7.03.09: **34**-46-95

This compilation marked the end of Annie's recording contract with Sony BMG.

'It seems the time has come,' she said, 'to release The Collection this year. The songs are timeless, and have become classics in their own right.'

Annie included two new songs on the album, both covers: *Shining Light* and *Pattern Of My Life*.

Shining Light was originally recorded by Ash, for their 2001 album, *FREE ALL ANGELS*. *Pattern Of My Life*, originally titled *Call Me What You Like*, was recorded by Keane, and was released as the B-side of their 2000 single, *Closer Now*.

Shining Light was released as a single, and achieved Top 40 status, just, in the UK only. *Pattern Of My Life* was only released digitally, and as a promo single, but it wasn't a hit anywhere.

THE ANNIE LENNOX COLLECTION charted at no.2 in the UK, no.4 in New Zealand and Norway, no.10 in Australia, no.15 in Germany, no.23 in Switzerland, no.25 in the Netherlands, no.27 in Austria, no.34 in the USA and no.41 in Belgium.

19 ~ A CHRISTMAS CORNUCOPIA

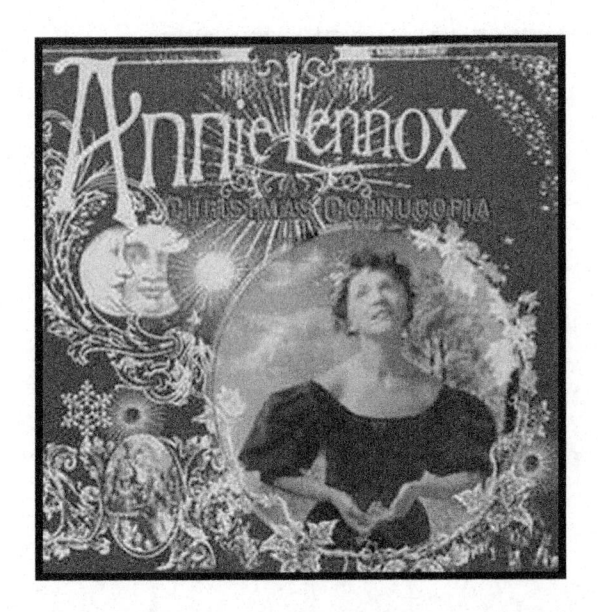

Angels From The Realms Of Glory/God Rest Ye Merry Gentlemen/See Amid The Winter's Snow/Il Est Ne Le Divin Enfant/The First Noel/Lullay Lullay (The Coventry Carol)/The Holly And The Ivy/In The Bleak Midwinter/As Joseph Was A Walking (The Cherry Tree Carol)/O Little Town Of Bethlehem/Silent Night/Universal Child

Produced by Annie Lennox & Mike Stevens.

UK: Island Records 2753311 (2010).

27.11.10: 27-38-29-18-18-**16**-86
24.12.11: 78-98

Australia
19.12.10: 86-84-**76**

Austria
10.12.10: 42-38-**35-35**-66

Belgium
1.01.11: **74**

Germany
26.11.10: 60-81-67-61-74-**37**-89

Annie Lennox
A Christmas Cornucopia

'Timeless holiday classics
from one of our most beloved icons
Featuring the new single
UNIVERSAL CHILD

Available November 16th

www.annielennox.com

Netherlands
18.12.10: 90-**60**-86

Norway
25.12.10: **38**

Sweden
26.11.10: 47-28-**24**-26-43-52

Switzerland
5.12.10: **38**-43-57-60-75

USA
4.12.10: 46-76-47-**35**-38-49

Annie's first and to date only Christmas album was recorded between October 2009 and the summer of 2010 at two studios, London's Sheen Lane and Milestone Studios in Cape Town, South Africa ~ several of the tracks featured The African Children's Choir.

Having departed Sony BMG, Annie signed for the Universal Music Group (Island in the UK, Decca in North America), and *A CHRISTMAS CORNUCOPIA* was her first album for her new label.

'I've known these songs, these carols, all my life,' she said. 'I've sung them since I was little. They're just in me. They're a huge part of my life, so it's not an arbitrary selection. Those relationships with those pieces of music were there intrinsically before I approached the recording.'

Annie wrote one new song for the album, *Universal Child*.

Universal Child and *God Rest Ye Merry Gentlemen* were both promoted as digital singles, and in the UK promo CD singles were issued, but neither single charted anywhere.

'All the income that I earn from *Universal Child*,' said Annie, 'will be paid to the Annie Lennox Foundation.'

The aim of the Foundation was to raise money for projects supporting and educating woman and children in Africa with HIV/AIDS.

The following Christmas, a third single *The Holy And The Ivy* was released digitally and as a promo CD single in the UK, but again it wasn't a hit.

A CHRISTMAS CORUCOPIA was a hit, albeit not on the same scale as Annie's earlier solo albums. The album achieved no.16 in the UK, no.24 in Sweden, no.35 in Austria and the USA, no.37 in Germany, and no.38 in Norway and Switzerland, and it was a minor hit in Australia, Belgium and the Netherlands.

20 ~ NOSTALGIA

Memphis In June/Georgia On My Mind/I Put A Spell On You/Summertime/I Cover The Waterfront/Strange Fruit/God Bless The Child/You Belong To Me/September In The Rain/I Can Dream, Can't I?/The Nearness Of You/Mood Indigo

Deluxe Edition Bonus DVD: Annie Lennox discusses *NOSTALGIA*/*I Put A Spell On You (Live)*

Produced by Annie Lennox & Mike Stevens.

UK: Blue Note Records/Island Records 4705576 (2014).

8.11.14: **9**-10-21-30-36-29-24-24-35-63-60-74

Australia
16.11.14: **16**-37-71-x-x-x-x-85-92

Austria
7.11.14: **10**-11-29-65

Belgium
8.11.14: **45**-67-100

France
8.11.14: **75**

ORIGIN.
The Conscious Lifestyle Magazine

Gloria STEINEM
EQUAL RIGHTS

GIFTS WE LOVE
CLOTHING ◂
JEWELRY ◂
SKINCARE ◂
GEAR ◂

VEGAN FOODS FOR WINTER

FARM TO TABLE

Arianna HUFFINGTON
THRIVING ◂

Redefining SUCCESS
MICHAEL FRANTI
JOHN MACKEY
▸ MOBY
KEN WILBER

ANNIE LENNOX
NOSTALGIA + POWERFUL WOMEN

ROBIN LIM
MIDWIFE + PHILIPPINES

OXFAM
THE WATER CRISIS

AYURVEDA. TANTRA. EMOTIONS.

Germany
7.11.14: **15**-49-73

Netherlands
1.11.14: **34**-75-97

New Zealand
10.11.14: **29**

Norway
8.04.14: **25**-x-x-**25**

Spain
2.11.14: **70**-75-97

Sweden
5.12.14: 46-52-**34**-58

Switzerland
2.11.14: **8**-33-34-61-x-98

USA
8.11.14: **10**-23-46-56-98

Her most recent album, *NOSTALGIA* was Annie's sixth solo studio album, and her third album of covers. Most of the songs Annie chose to record date from the 1930s to the 1950s.

'At this point in time,' she said, 'less is more for me. I'm more about quality than quantity, and I think this is quite a niche place to be.'

I Put A Spell On You was chosen as the album's lead single. It wasn't a hit in the UK, but it did chart in several countries, most notably France where it rose to no.29.

Annie performed *I Put A Spell On You* at the 57th Annual Grammy Awards, where *NOSTALGIA* picked up a nomination for Best Traditional Pop Vocal Album, but Annie lost out to Tony Bennett & Lady Gaga's *CHEEK TO CHEEK*. *I Put A Spell On You* also featured in the 2015 film, *Fifty Shades Of Grey*.

Summertime and *Georgia On My Mind* were also promoted as digital singles in the UK, but like *I Put A Spell On You*, they both failed to chart.

EMMA

www.emma.de

DIÄTEN & SEX
Das hängt zusammen!

DIE BURKA
Verbot in Deutschland?

PUFFS & PÄDOS
in Schulbüchern

BORDELL-RAZZIA!
Und das neue Gesetz?

Wie richtig altern?

ANNIE LENNOX, 60

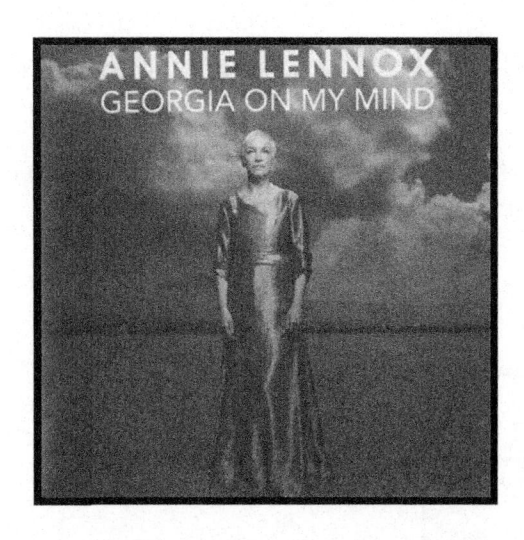

NOSTALGIA charted at no.8 in Switzerland, no.9 in the UK, no.10 in Austria and the USA, no.15 in Germany, no.16 in Australia, no.25 in Norway, no.29 in New Zealand, no.34 in the Netherlands and Sweden, and no.45 in Belgium.

In the United States, *NOSTALGIA* went all the way to no.1 on Billboards Jazz Albums and Traditional Jazz Albums charts.

ANNIE'S TOP 20 ALBUMS

This Top 20 Albums listing has been compiled using the same points system as for Annie's Top 30 Singles listing.

Rank/Album/Points

1 *GREATEST HITS* – 2155 points

2 *REVENGE* – 2128 points

3 *BE YOURSELF TONIGHT* – 1917 points

Rank/Album/Points

4 *MEDUSA* – 1668 points

5 *DIVA* – 1538 points

6. *WE TOO ARE ONE* – 1476 points
7. *TOUCH* – 1293 points
8. *PEACE* – 1190 points
9. *SWEET DREAMS (ARE MADE OF THIS)* – 1183 points
10. *SAVAGE* – 1095 points

11. *BARE* – 948 points
12. *ULTIMATE COLLECTION* – 929 points
13. *NOSTALGIA* – 776 points
14. *THE ANNIE LENNOX COLLECTION* – 763 points
15. *SONGS OF MASS DESTRUCTION* – 651 points

16. *1984 (FOR THE LOVE OF BIG BROTHER)* – 629 points
17. *A CHRISTMAS CORNUCOPIA* – 471 points
18. *REALITY EFFECT* – 218 points
19. *LIVE 1983-1989* – 150 points
20. *TOUCH DANCE* – 55 points

Eurythmics take the Top 3 places, with *GREATEST HITS* proving the duo's most successful album, narrowly ahead of *REVENGE* and *BE YOURSELF TONIGHT*. Solo, Annie's *MEDUSA* and *DIVA* albums round off the Top 5.

The only Tourists album to make the Top 20, *REALITY EFFECT*, is at no.18.

ALBUMS TRIVIA

To date, Annie Lennox ~ solo, and with The Tourists & Eurythmics ~ has achieved twenty Top 40 albums: 12 with Eurythmics, seven solo and one as part of The Tourists. There follows a country-by-country look at her most successful albums.

ANNIE IN AUSTRALIA

Most Hits

10 hits	Eurythmics
7 hits	Annie Lennox
1 hit	The Tourists

Most Weeks

313 weeks	Eurythmics
72 weeks	Annie Lennox
5 weeks	The Tourists

No.1 Albums

1985	*BE YOURSELF TONIGHT*
1991	*GREATEST HITS*

Most weeks at No.1

6 weeks	*GREATEST HITS*
4 weeks	*BE YOURSELF TONIGHT*

Most Weeks

58 weeks	*REVENGE*
54 weeks	*BE YOURSELF TONIGHT*
46 weeks	*GREATEST HITS*
37 weeks	*TOUCH*
32 weeks	*SWEET DREAMS (ARE MADE OF THIS)*
29 weeks	*WE TOO ARE ONE*
26 weeks	*DIVA*
23 weeks	*SAVAGE*
17 weeks	*ULTIMATE COLLECTION*

13 weeks   *1984 (FOR THE LOVE OF BIG BROTHER)*
13 weeks   *THE ANNIE LENNOX COLLECTION*

ANNIE IN AUSTRIA

Most Hits

8 hits   Eurythmics
7 hits   Annie Lennox

Most weeks

93 weeks   Eurythmics
57 weeks   Annie Lennox

No.1 Albums

1991   *GREATEST HITS*

GREATEST HITS topped the chart for two weeks.

Albums with the most Weeks

36 weeks   *REVENGE*
26 weeks   *GREATEST HITS*
16 weeks   *DIVA*
16 weeks   *MEDUSA*
11 weeks   *PEACE*

ANNIE IN BELGIUM (Flanders)

Most Hits

6 hits   Annie Lennox
2 hits   Eurythmics

Most weeks

34 weeks   Annie Lennox
23 weeks   Eurythmics

Annie's most successful album since 1995 in Belgium (Flanders) is *MEDUSA*, which peaked at no.8.

Albums with the most Weeks

23 weeks   *ULTIMATE COLLECTION*
17 weeks   *MEDUSA*
 7 weeks   *THE ANNIE LENNOX COLLECTION*

Note: this information relates to 1995 onwards only.

ANNIE IN CANADA

Most Hits

9 hits   Eurythmics
2 hits   Annie Lennox
1 hit   The Tourists

Most weeks

324 weeks   Eurythmics
111 weeks   Annie Lennox
  5 weeks   The Tourists

No.1 Albums

1995   *MEDUSA*

MEDUSA topped the chart for one week.

Albums with the most Weeks

64 weeks   *DIVA*
49 weeks   *SWEET DREAMS (ARE MADE OF THIS)*
48 weeks   *BE YOURSELF TONIGHT*
47 weeks   *MEDUSA*
44 weeks   *TOUCH*
43 weeks   *REVENGE*
36 weeks   *WE TOO ARE ONE*
33 weeks   *GREATEST HITS*
31 weeks   *SAVAGE*

20 weeks   *1984 (FOR THE LOVE OF BIG BROTHER)*
20 weeks   *PEACE*

Note: this information relates to pre-2000 only.

ANNIE IN FINLAND

Most Hits

7 hits   Eurythmics
2 hits   Annie Lennox

Most Weeks

102 weeks   Eurythmics
 27 weeks   Annie Lennox

No.1 Albums

1986   *REVENGE*

REVENGE topped the chart for two weeks.

Most weeks

37 weeks   *REVENGE*
21 weeks   *BE YOURSELF TONIGHT*
17 weeks   *GREATEST HITS*
17 weeks   *DIVA*
10 weeks   *SAVAGE*
10 weeks   *WE TOO ARE ONE*
10 weeks   *MEDUSA*

ANNIE IN FRANCE

Most Hits

7 hits   Eurythmics
5 hits   Annie Lennox

Most weeks

67 weeks   Eurythmics
30 weeks   Annie Lennox

No.1 Albums

1991   *GREATEST HITS*

GREATEST HITS topped the chart for four weeks.

Albums with the most weeks

17 weeks   *MEDUSA*
16 weeks   *REVENGE*
14 weeks   *WE TOO ARE ONE*
12 weeks   *GREATEST HITS*
12 weeks   *PEACE*

ANNIE IN GERMANY

Most Hits

11 hits   Eurythmics
 7 hits   Annie Lennox

Most Weeks

261 weeks   Eurythmics
 98 weeks   Annie Lennox

No.1 Albums

1991   *GREATEST HITS*

GREATEST HITS topped the chart for one week.

Albums with the most weeks

54 weeks   *GREATEST HITS*
38 weeks   *REVENGE*
37 weeks   *DIVA*
34 weeks   *WE TOO ARE ONE*

33 weeks	*BE YOURSELF TONIGHT*
25 weeks	*MEDUSA*
23 weeks	*SWEET DREAMS (ARE MADE OF THIS)*
21 weeks	*PEACE*
20 weeks	*TOUCH*
14 weeks	*SAVAGE*

ANNIE IN JAPAN

Most Hits

9 hits   Eurythmics

Most Weeks

31 weeks   Eurythmics

Annie's most successful album in Japan is *WE TOO ARE ONE*, which peaked at no.38.

Most weeks on the chart

6 weeks	*BE YOURSELF TONIGHT*
6 weeks	*GREATEST HITS*
5 weeks	*1984 (FOR THE LOVE OF BIG BROTHER)*
5 weeks	*REVENGE*
5 weeks	*WE TOO ARE ONE*

ANNIE IN THE NETHERLANDS

Most Hits

11 hits	Eurythmics
7 hits	Annie Lennox

Most Weeks

239 weeks	Eurythmics
86 weeks	Annie Lennox

No.1 Albums

1991   *GREATEST HITS*

GREATEST HITS topped the chart for six straight weeks.

Albums with the most weeks

45 weeks	*BE YOURSELF TONIGHT*
38 weeks	*GREATEST HITS*
30 weeks	*TOUCH*
30 weeks	*REVENGE*
28 weeks	*SWEET DREAMS (ARE MADE OF THIS)*
27 weeks	*MEDUSA*
25 weeks	*DIVA*
23 weeks	*ULTIMATE COLLECTION*
16 weeks	*BARE*
15 weeks	*PEACE*

ANNIE IN NEW ZEALAND

Most Hits

9 hits	Eurythmics
5 hits	Annie Lennox

Most Weeks

246 weeks	Eurythmics
64 weeks	Annie Lennox

No.1 Albums

1987	*REVENGE*
1991	*GREATEST HITS*

Most weeks at No.1

10 weeks	*REVENGE*
8 weeks	*GREATEST HITS*

Most weeks

48 weeks	*REVENGE*
47 weeks	*BE YOURSELF TONIGHT*
41 weeks	*SWEET DREAMS (ARE MADE OF THIS)*
31 weeks	*TOUCH*

27 weeks   *GREATEST HITS*
27 weeks   *DIVA*
25 weeks   *SAVAGE*
15 weeks   *MEDUSA*
12 weeks   *THE ANNIE LENNOX COLLECTION*
10 weeks   *ULTIMATE COLLECTION*

ANNIE IN NORWAY

Most Hits

8 hits   Eurythmics
6 hits   Annie Lennox

Most Weeks

117 weeks   Eurythmics
 36 weeks   Annie Lennox

No.1 Albums

1986   *REVENGE*

REVENGE topped the chart for six weeks.

Albums with the most weeks

35 weeks   *REVENGE*
27 weeks   *BE YOURSELF TONIGHT*
22 weeks   *GREATEST HITS*
20 weeks   *MEDUSA*
17 weeks   *TOUCH*

ANNIE IN SOUTH AFRICA

Most Hits

6 hits   Eurythmics
1 hit   Annie Lennox

Most Weeks

74 weeks   Eurythmics
 9 weeks   Annie Lennox

Annie's most successful album in South Africa is *GREATEST HITS*, which peaked at no.2.

Albums with the most weeks

27 weeks   *GREATEST HITS*
17 weeks   *BE YOURSELF TONIGHT*
13 weeks   *WE TOO ARE ONE*
11 weeks   *TOUCH*
 9 weeks   *DIVA*

ANNIE IN SPAIN

Most Hits

7 hits   Eurythmics
4 hits   Annie Lennox

Most Weeks

87 weeks   Eurythmics
37 weeks   Annie Lennox

Annie's most successful album in Spain is *GREATEST HITS*, which peaked at no.4.

Most Weeks

30 weeks   *GREATEST HITS*
21 weeks   *MEDUSA*
16 weeks   *REVENGE*
13 weeks   *WE TOO ARE ONE*
12 weeks   *SWEET DREAMS (ARE MADE OF THIS)*
12 weeks   *DIVA*

ANNIE IN SWEDEN

Most Hits

10 hits	Eurythmics
6 hits	Annie Lennox
1 hit	The Tourists

Most Weeks

204 weeks	Eurythmics
72 weeks	Annie Lennox
2 weeks	The Tourists

No.1 Albums

1986	*REVENGE*
1989	*WE TOO ARE ONE*

Most weeks at No.1

12 weeks	*REVENGE*
2 weeks	*WE TOO ARE ONE*

Most weeks on the chart

36 weeks	*BE YOURSELF TONIGHT*
31 weeks	*MEDUSA*
28 weeks	*REVENGE*
24 weeks	*TOUCH*
24 weeks	*DIVA*
22 weeks	*SWEET DREAMS (ARE MADE OF THIS)*
22 weeks	*GREATEST HITS*
18 weeks	*WE TOO ARE ONE*
16 weeks	*1984 (FOR THE LOVE OF BIG BROTHER)*
14 weeks	*ULTIMATE COLLECTION*

ANNIE IN SWITZERLAND

Most Hits

9 hits	Eurythmics
7 hits	Annie Lennox

Most Weeks

132 weeks   Eurythmics
 74 weeks   Annie Lennox

Annie's most successful albums in Switzerland are *WE TOO ARE ONE*, *GREATEST HITS* and *PEACE*, which all peaked at no.2.

Albums with the most weeks

34 weeks   *REVENGE*
24 weeks   *GREATEST HITS*
22 weeks   *DIVA*
20 weeks   *BE YOURSELF TONIGHT*
19 weeks   *MEDUSA*
16 weeks   *PEACE*
13 weeks   *WE TOO ARE ONE*
12 weeks   *BARE*

ANNIE IN THE UNITED KINGDOM

Most Hits

12 hits   Eurythmics
 7 hits   Annie Lennox
 3 hits   The Tourists

Most Weeks

561 weeks   Eurythmics
216 weeks   Annie Lennox
 18 weeks   The Tourists

No.1 Albums

1983   *TOUCH*
1989   *WE TOO ARE ONE*
1991   *GREATEST HITS*
1992   *DIVA*
1995   *MEDUSA*

Most weeks at No.1

10 weeks	*GREATEST HITS*
2 weeks	*TOUCH*
2 weeks	*DIVA*

Albums with the most Weeks

159 weeks	*GREATEST HITS*
95 weeks	*DIVA*
80 weeks	*BE YOURSELF TONIGHT*
60 weeks	*SWEET DREAMS (ARE MADE OF THIS)*
54 weeks	*MEDUSA*
52 weeks	*REVENGE*
48 weeks	*TOUCH*
46 weeks	*ULTIMATE COLLECTION*
33 weeks	*SAVAGE*
32 weeks	*WE TOO ARE ONE*

BRIT Certified/BPI (British Phonographic Industry) Awards

The BPI began certifying albums in 1973, and between April 1973 and December 1978, awards related to a monetary value and not a unit value. When this system was abolished, the awards that were set remain in place today: Silver = 60,000, Gold = 100,000, Platinum = 300,000. Multi-Platinum awards were introduced in February 1987.

In July 2013 the BPI automated awards, and awards from this date are based on actual sales since February 1994, not shipments.

6 x Platinum	*GREATEST HITS* (May 1993) = 1.8 million
4 x Platinum	*DIVA* (January 1995) = 1.2 million
3 x Platinum	*ULTIMATE COLLECTION* (July 2013) = 900,000
2 x Platinum	*BE YOURSELF TONIGHT* (February 1986) = 600,000
2 x Platinum	*REVENGE* (January 1987) = 600,000
2 x Platinum	*WE TOO ARE ONE* (June 1990) = 600,000
2 x Platinum	*MEDUSA* (October 1995) = 600,000
Platinum	*TOUCH* (January 1984) = 300,000
Platinum	*SWEET DREAMS (ARE MADE OF THIS)* (January 1984) = 300,000
Platinum	*SAVAGE* (November 1987) = 300,000
Platinum	*THE COLLECTION* (July 2013) = 300,000
Gold	*1984* (December 1984) = 100,000
Gold	*LIVE 1983-89* (December 1993) = 100,000
Gold	*PEACE* (November 1999) = 100,000

Gold	*BARE* (October 2003) = 100,000
Gold	*A CHRISTMAS CORNUCOPIA* (December 2010) = 100,000
Gold	*NOSTALGIA* (January 2015) = 100,000
Silver	*REALITY EFFECT* (January 1980) = 60,000
Silver	*SONGS OF MASS DESTRUCTION* (July 2013) = 60,000

ANNIE IN THE UNITED STATES OF AMERICA

Most Hits

9 hits	Eurythmics

Most Weeks

196 weeks	Eurythmics
121 weeks	Annie Lennox

Annie's most successful album in the USA is *TOUCH*, which peaked at no.7.

Albums with the most Weeks

54 weeks	*DIVA*
46 weeks	*SWEET DREAMS (ARE MADE OF THIS)*
36 weeks	*BE YOURSELF TONIGHT*
34 weeks	*TOUCH*
34 weeks	*MEDUSA*
24 weeks	*REVENGE*
23 weeks	*WE TOO ARE ONE*
14 weeks	*BARE*
12 weeks	*SAVAGE*
12 weeks	*GREATEST HITS*

RIAA (Recording Industry Association of America) Awards

The RIAA began certifying Gold albums in 1958, Platinum albums in 1976, and multi-Platinum albums in 1984. Gold = 500,000, Platinum = 1 million. Awards are based on shipments, not sales, and each disc is counted individually (so, for example, a double album has to ship 500,000 to be eligible for Platinum).

3 x Platinum	*GREATEST HITS* (February 1999) = 3 million
2 x Platinum	*DIVA* (August 1996) = 2 million
2 x Platinum	*MEDUSA* (June 1998) = 2 million

Platinum	*TOUCH* (October 1984)	= 1 million
Platinum	*BE YOURSELF TONIGHT* (September 1985)	= 1 million
Gold	*SWEET DREAMS (ARE MADE OF THIS)* (November 1983)	= 500,000
Gold	*REVENGE* (September 1986)	= 500,000
Gold	*PEACE* (November 1999)	= 500,000
Gold	*BARE* (July 2003)	= 500,000

ANNIE IN ZIMBABWE

Most Hits

4 hits	Eurythmics
1 hit	Annie Lennox
1 hit	The Tourists

Annie's most successful albums in Zimbabwe are *TOUCH* and *BE YOURSELF TONIGHT*, which both peaked at no.3.

Printed in Great Britain
by Amazon